Sunday's Open House Anthology

Edited by

Abiodun Oyewole
of
The Last Poets

Published by Human Error Publishing
www.humanerrorpublishing.com
paul@humanerrorpublishing.com

Copyright 2025
by
Human Error Publishing
and
Abiodun Oyewole

All Rights Reserved

ISBN: 978-1-948521-23-9

Editing & Cover Design
Abiodun Oyewole
&
Human Error Publishing

The door photo front cover is Juanita Jackson aka Queen Jua
The photo of Abiodun Back Cover is Verleen Killz of Killz Blog Studios

All poems submitted by the authors in this book are owned and copyrighted by each individual author and remain theirs. HEP thanks each author for including their work here.

Human Error Publishing asks that no part of this publication be reproduced or transmitted in any form or by any means electronic or mechanical, including photocopy, recording or information storage or retrieval system without permission in writing from Abiodun Oyewole and Human Error Publishing. The reasons for this are to help support publisher and the artists.

Table of Contents

The Pledge	7
History Sunday Open House	8
Abiodun Oyewole	10
Enid Pickett	19
Agu, Prince Osinayah - happyprince	29
Vernon C. Robinson (VCR)	37
Ishmael Street	48
Elemen2al The Poet	51
Paul Richmond	59
Devynity	70
Karega Ani	76
a g	85
Baba Ngoma Osayemi Ifatunmise	88
Osunyoyin Alake Ifarike	98
George "LiteSkin" Escalante	109
Juanita Queen Jua	120
Charles Perry Jr. :: CP Maze	131
Rewop Be	134
CeLillianne Green	143
Toni Hamilton	151
K'larity St John	159
Tasha Jones	170
Pharoah Davis	177
The Pledge	188

The pledge came about ten years after the Open House had started. It became the opening because it worked well with the students I was working with. The pledge was a freestyle because I don't do the pledge to the flag nor sing the war song anthem. I was called out at a speaking engagement by a young girl. I told her and the audience I had a much better pledge than the pledge of allegiance. An elder woman in the audience asked to hear my pledge. The truth is I hadn't written it, but I was planning to. I responded by saying "sure". The pledge was born. It was performed very slowly because I was thinking it while I was saying it.

The Pledge is recited before and after every Sunday's Open House

The Pledge

I want to be what I can be
To be proud, healthy and FREE
I want to say what I know
To help my brothers and sisters GROW
I want to feel good about me
And blame no one for my MISERY
I'll be strong, turn it around
I want to go up, I'm not going DOWN
I want to do what I can do
To make all my dreams come TRUE
Remember my past, the good and bad
How I make art, even when it was SAD
I want to share whatever my gift
And when you're feeling low I'll give you A LIFT
I want to live without FEAR
And know that I'm blessed for being HERE
And know that you're blessed for being HERE
And know that we're blessed for being HERE
And know that we are BLESSED

Abiodun Oyewole

Abiodun's History of the Sunday Gathering

POETRY OPEN HOUSE

Open House at 110 Morningside Drive started over forty years ago. I didn't plan it. It really just happened. Every Sunday I would take my sons and friends to Columbia's gym to play basketball. Since I was teaching there, I had access to the gym and other facilities. The rule was I could only invite two guests. I would bring as many as fifteen guests on any given Sunday. One Sunday a new guest joined us. He was an admirer of my poetry and wanted to share a poem he had written. Because I was so caught up in playing basketball, I told the young man I didn't have time to hear his poem and told him we were going to play some poetry.

He knew I was a member of The Last Poets and wanted my opinion of his poetry. We played basketball with the young man on my team. We had a winning day. When we were getting ready to leave the gym, I told the young man he could read the poem. He reached into his pocket, pulled out a folded piece of paper and opened it up. The poem was replaced by blotches of blue ink. The sweat from playing ball had erased his poem. He looked devastated. I felt responsible because I refused to listen to it when we first met. I put my hands on his shoulder and told him I was going to take him to my house and let him sit at my desk to rewrite his poem. I also told him that I would fix some food for him to eat. He made an effort to rewrite the poem. He said that he remembered about ninety percent of it. When he shared it with me I was impressed. I gave him some constructive criticism and he appeared to be satisfied.

Every Sunday from then on was basketball and poetry. I discovered a few of my ball buddies were budding poets as well. My Sundays became a routine of me getting up early and preparing food before we played basketball. The menu was always the same salmon croquettes, grits, scrambled eggs, home fries and apple or orange juice. Later I added fried apples to the menu. My mother once said people were not coming to my house to read poetry. They were coming to eat free food. It was a chore, but a necessary one that encouraged a lot of young artists to develop their craft.

The Open House would provide poets, singers, musicians, playwrights and dancers a platform to present their gifts

Abiodun Oyewole

BLACK HISTORY

IN THE BEGINNING
THERE WAS BLACKNESS
FROM THAT BLACKNESS CAME THE LIGHT
EVERYTHING THAT LIVED
CAME OUT OF BLACKNESS
EVERY COLOR
EVERY FLAVOR
EVERY SOUND
EVERY HEARTBEAT
EVERY WORD
EVERY THOUGHT
EVERY DREAM
CAME FROM BLACKNESS
WE THE MELANATED ONES
REFLECT THAT BLACKNESS
IN OUR SKIN
IN OUR ENERGY
IN OUR LOVE
BEYOND THE BODY AND MIND
THERE IS A SPIRIT
THE SPIRIT IS THE LIGHT OF BLACKNESS
IT SHOWS US THE PATH
THAT WE MUST FOLLOW
THERE HAVE BEEN MANY KEEPERS OF THE LIGHT
THEY WERE ALL BLACK
JESUS JEWS MARY MOSES ABRAHAM SARAH DAVID
THEIR DEEDS WERE SO GREAT
THEY WERE GIVEN PRAISE
STORIES WERE WRITTEN ABOUT THEM
ALTARS WERE CREATED
SO THEY WOULD BE REVERED
TEMPLES AND CHURCHES
MONASTERIES AND CATHEDRALS
ERECTED IN THEIR HONOR

BUT LIFE IS A SERIES OF LESSONS
MAN IS A FOREVER STUDENT
MISTAKES WILL BE MADE
CONFLICTS WILL OCCUR
PEACE WILL NOT REIGN SUPREME
LYING AND STEALING AND KILLING
WILL BE CHRONIC GERMS
TO INVADE THE SOUL OF MAN
EVERYTHING WILL CHANGE
WE ARE LIVING IN THAT CHANGE
TRYING TO GET BACK
TO THE WAY THINGS WERE
IT WILL TAKE SOME TIME
WE WILL RETURN

ART

ART IS THE REFLECTION OF THE GOD
THAT LIVES INSIDE OF US
THE CREATIVE VEIN THAT CONNECTS
TO THE SOUL
THE VERY HEART OF OUR DREAMS AND DESIRES
THE TRUE EXPRESSION OF SELF
AT ITS HIGHEST ORDER
EACH ONE OF US IS A VERSION
OF THE ART OF GOD
WE TRY TO IMITATE THE ENERGY
THAT MADE US
WE TRY TO DUPLICATE THE CREATOR
IN ALL THAT WE CREATE
ART IS THE MIRROR OF OUR LOVE
WHAT WE SEE AND FEEL IS SACRED
IT IS THE IMMORTALITY OF US
RELICS OF HEAVEN
JEWELS OF HUMANITY
TELLING STORIES OF WHAT WAS
WHAT IS
WHAT'S YET TO COME
WITHOUT ART
LIFE WOULD NOT HAVE A PULSE
MAN WOULD ALWAYS BE LONELY
MAN HAS MADE MACHINES TO CREATE ART
TECHNICAL ART TO FEED OUR PASSION
REPLACE THE BLOOD WITH ELECTRICAL CURRENTS
DESIGNED TO TOUCH OUR SOUL
MOTHER NATURE IS THE SUPREME ARTIST
HER TREES AND FLOWERS
MOUNTAINS AND VALLEYS
RIVERS AND WATERFALLS
DESERTS AND MEADOWS
DECORATE THE LANDSCAPE OF THIS PLANET
WE SPEND A LIFETIME
TRYING TO CATCH UP WITH MOTHER NATURE
ART IS THE PRAYER OF HER BLESSINGS

JOY

JOY IS REVOLUTION
WHEN MISERY BECOMES
THE ONLY MEAL ON THE MENU
HATE IS THE TASTE ON YOUR TONGUE
WHEN DISEASE AND SICKNESS
COME IN THE MAIL
OVER THE PHONE
ON TV TALK SHOWS
POLITICAL DISCUSSIONS
GENERAL CONVERSATIONS
JOY IS REVOLUTION
WE SPEND DAYS AND NIGHTS
TO STOP DROWNING
FROM A TIDAL WAVE OF DISAPPOINTMENTS
AN AVALANCHE OF GRIEF
A PLANE CRASH OF HOPES
COLLIDING IN THE SKY
THE VERY AIR WE BREATHE
HAS BECOME SUSPECT
TO OUR WELL BEING
A SURGICAL MASK BECOMES
PART OF OUR DAILY ATTIRE
JOY IS REVOLUTION
WHEN GOD IS PROSTITUTED
TO MAKE MONEY FOR MINISTERS
TO BUY A NEW CAR
TAKE VACATIONS IN THE BAHAMAS
GIVE THE PEOPLE BANDAIDS
FOR A CHRONIC DISEASE
JOY IS REVOLUTION
WHEN SHE STANDS ON ROOFTOPS
ARMS STRETCHED OUT
PRAISING GOD FOR OUR BLESSINGS
DELIVERANCE FROM EVIL
OR WALKING ALONG THE SHORE
BAREFOOT IN THE WATER
ANOINTING OUR SOULS
WITH REDEMPTION

REMEMBERING OUR ANCESTORS
JOY IS HEARING THE BABY GIGGLE
WATCHING THE CHILDREN PLAY
LISTENING TO GOOD MUSIC
CREATING AN EXPRESSION OF ART
WATCHING FRIENDS GREETING
HUGGING WITH SINCERE FEELINGS
SLAPPING HIGH FIVE WITH CONFIDENCE
WE GOT IT LIKE THAT
JOY IS DANCING IN THE STREET
SINGING ON THE SUBWAY
PLAYING CONGAS IN THE PARK
SMILING AT THE PEOPLE PASSING BY
JOY IS A BREATH OF FRESH AIR
NO MORE BILLS TO PAY
LIVING RENT FREE
GROWING FOOD IN YOUR BACKYARD
EMBRACING YOUR CULTURE
APPRECIATING WHO YOU ARE
GUNS ARE IN THE MUSEUM
WAR NO LONGER EXIST
LOVE IS A WAY OF LIFE
PEACE IS SUNRISE AND SUNSET
JOY IS REVOLUTION

UNDER THE LAKES

A CHANCE TO LIVE
TO CREATE A PLACE
THAT WE COULD CALL HOME
DIDN'T LAST TOO LONG
BEFORE THINGS WENT WRONG
WHITE FOLKS WERE UPSET
WHAT BLACKS HAD THEY COULDN'T GET
THEY WERE SICK WITH JEALOUSY
BLACKS LIVING GOOD
THIS JUST COULDN'T BE
SO THEY KILLED AND THEY BURNED
EVERYTHING WE EARNED
DUG GRAVEYARDS SO DEEP
YOU COULD BURY A TOWN
FLOODED THE TOWN WITH WATER
SO DREAMS AND MEMORIES WOULD DROWN
TURNED THE TOWN INTO A LAKE
TO COVER THEIR VICIOUS ATTACKS
THE SPIRITS STAYED AWAKE
SOUGHT REVENGE FOR THE BLACKS
YOU COULD HEAR THE ANCESTORS BREATHING
PLAYING THE DRUMS UNDER WATER
THEY WERE THERE TO PROTECT
THEIR SONS AND THEIR DAUGHTERS
THE LAKE HAS A SOUL
THAT CANNOT BE DESTROYED
KARMA IS SOMETHING
NO ONE CAN AVOID
MANY YEARS HAVE PASSED
PEOPLE ARE DROWNING IN THE LAKE
THE ANCESTORS DOWN THERE
ARE CHOOSING BODIES THEY SHOULD TAKE
NO ONE SEEMS TO UNDERSTAND
THIS STRANGE MYSTERY
IT'S JUST ANOTHER LESSON
IN BLACK HISTORY

DANCE WITH ME

DANCE WITH ME
LET'S PLAY SOME MUSIC
BE FREE FOR AWHILE
DANCE TOGETHER
BE IN RHYTHM
WITH EACH OTHER
BODIES MOVING IN HARMONY
YOU SEE THE MUSIC IN US
EACH STEP WE TAKE IS LIKE A MUSICAL NOTE
LIKE WE'VE BEEN PRACTICING
HOW TO BE IN TUNE
DANCE WITH ME
TAKE MY HAND
LET ME TURN YOU
LET ME LOVE YOU IN THIS MOMENT
GOT ME SMILING
JUST TO WATCH HOW
SASSY YOU MOVE IN MY ARMS
LIKE YOU KNOW YOU GOT ME
AND I GOT YOU
DANCE WITH ME
FORGET ABOUT THE TROUBLES
OF THE WORLD
FOR A MOMENT LET'S TAKE FLIGHT
CREATE STEPS TO TAKE US HIGHER
ABOVE THE MISERY AND MADNESS
LET OUR DANCING TAKE US
TO A PLACE WHERE HAPPINESS IS LIVING
LIVING IS ALL THAT REALLY MATTERS
NOT HAVING MONEY
NOT FIGHTING
NOT BEING WITHOUT
LET'S DANCE LIKE WE'VE DISCOVERED
THE TRUE TREASURE OF TIME AND SPACE
LET'S ENJOY EACH OTHER
CELEBRATE OUR HEART BODY AND SOUL

MUSIC

MUSIC IS POURING HONEY ON LANGUAGE
MAKING SOUNDS EMBRACING PASSION
TO INSPIRE OUR SOULS TO SMILE
MUSIC IS AN INTIMATE LOVER
LYING NAKED BESIDE US
CARESSING THE FEELINGS OF YOUR HEART
MUSIC GIVES WINGS TO YOUR IMAGINATION
PROVIDES THE DAY WITH COLOR
CREATE A SONG
TO MAKE THE TONGUE AND THROAT DANCE
IN THE AIR
SO LIFE CAN BREATHE
MUSIC BECOMES A PRAYER
WITH A MELODY TO ENCHANT YOUR THOUGHTS
A SWEET TASTE IN YOUR EARS
TO SATISFY YOUR CRAVINGS
THE MAESTRO OF YOUR HEART BEAT
CONDUCTING THE RHYTHM
OF EVERY STEP WE TAKE
PERSUADING OUR BODY TO DANCE
MUSIC IS THE NATURAL FRUIT
TO NOURISH OUR CREATION
AN ATTEMPT TO TALK TO GOD
OFFERS FREEDOM FROM THE MUNDANE
EXCITEMENT FROM THE ORDINARY
A PATHWAY TO JOY
WE CAN USE MUSIC TO HEAL THE HURT
TO UNITE THE PEOPLE
TO FIND A WAY TO LIVE IN PEACE
BRING COMFORT TO OUR SOULS
MAKE WAR OBSOLETE

Abiodun Oyewole (born Charles Davis, February 1948), is a poet, teacher and member of the African-American music and spoken-word group *The Last Poets*, which developed into what is considered to be the first hip hop group. Critic Jason Ankeny wrote, "With their politically charged raps, taut rhythms, and dedication to raising African-American consciousness, the Last Poets almost single-handedly laid the groundwork for the emergence of hip-hop."

Over the course of his forty year career and his long affiliation with The Last Poets, Oyewole is one of several poets credited for liberating American poetry by creating open, vocal, spontaneous, energetic and uncensored vernacular verse that paved the way for spoken word and Hip Hop. Using the spiritual, the sacred and the mystical, Oyewole often turns to the tree as a symbol of change and growth. His poetry re-branches into different directions, becoming grandeur in its proportions, and more complexly diversified in its structure.

Books by Abiodun

On A Mission:
Selected Poems and a History of the Last Poets
by Abiodun Oyewole, Umar Bin Hassan

Branches of the Tree of Life: The Collected Poems of Abiodun Oyewole, 1969-2013

NAKED: A New Poetry Collection Paperback – November 1, 2020 -by Abiodun Oyewole, Lyah Beth Leflore (Introduction)

LEGACY: A Book of Tributes - by Pharoah Oyewole Davis, Abiodun Oyewole

(2LP EXPLORATIONS)
Black Lives Have Always Mattered: A Collection of Essays, Poems, and Personal Narratives

Enid Pickett
Excerpts of Selected Poems

My Father

A simple, single, shadowed, shaded photo.
Black, white, gray.
Wrinkled, worn, weary like winter.
Standing center framed.
A tall lean "drink of water"
In dusty dry faded fatigues.
A Black & Proud World War II
U.S. Army Soldier
Planted in pounding passionate
Morning sunlight
On some forgotten beach…alone.
Before I was born.
A single photo, a single clue.
Priceless, lifelong mystery.
My Father.
A Ghost? A Secret?
A Myth? A Mist of Truth?
His name never
In anyone's mouth.
He was Invisible.
He was Incomparable.
He was Elusive…Until.
March 2021.
I found Him waiting to be Found.
Tangled in the middle of the World Wide Web.
You can find anything on the Internet.
It's true.
That Rabbit hole of DNA lives forever.
And ever.

John Buster Pickett

My Father is REAL.
He became my Velveteen Rabbit.
He became "REAL."
You see. "To become Real."
"It takes a long, long time.
That's why it doesn't happen to people who break easily.
Or, who have to be carefully kept.
Generally, by the time you are Real,
Most of your hair has been loved off.
And your eyes drop out,
you get loose in the joints and very shabby.
But those things don't matter at all,
Because once you are Real
You can't be ugly,
Except to people who don't understand."
I Understand.
I understand *who* You are.
I understand *what* You are.
I understand *why* You are.
I understand *where* You are.
I understand *now* You are.
I Understand.
I understand why fingers tingle when numb.
Feels like old knowledge made new.
I see You. I see Me.
I see John Buster Pickett.
You are REAL.
You are my father.
I Love You.
I Always will.

This...America

A Metamorphic Miracle.
Be Coming. Believing. Beginning.
Bountifully Brilliant
Being...America.

Her scars of the past cut deep into our DNA.
Her destiny dauntless.
Her memories guide the future with clear eyes & fairness.
She remembers the stolen deferred dreams of her ancestors.
She remembers the buried broken promises faded in the future.
She keeps her fingers crossed when she wishes on a star each night.
She smiles as she leaps into the Unknown unafraid.
Hoping. Praying. Holding on to the essence of eternal optimism.
Where all isms die in the sunlight of our ancestor's answers.
Her children sing songs of countless courage, lasting love & heartfelt hope.
Her children walk, run & play in egalitarian daydreams.
They live lives Liberty never imagined.
She parents her children with possibilities, passion & peace.
She wisely walks in whispering shoes.
Facing dangers fearlessly while sleeping with one eye open.
She conjures forgotten daydreams of the dead.
This...America.
A Metamorphic Miracle.
Be Coming. Believing. Beginning.
Bountifully Brilliant.
Being...America.

Armed with fierce vulnerabilities & multiple perspectives.
She holds Harmony in both hands.
Her best friend is named Hope.
Her innocence & Wisdom wrapped in melanated skins of compassion.
She shares intimate Organic Knowledge & Unapologetic Joy.
Trust & Truth twins keep her "feet to the fire."

She is gracefully strategic, mindfully compassionate
To live Free. To be Free.
Her story is old, and her story is not yet told.
"We too, sing America."
We too protect America.
We too, love & respect America.

This...is why the world believes.
This...is what the world daydreams.
This...Skin. This...Hair.
This...Face. This...Hope.
All are Metamorphic Miracles.
This...America, my home.

What kind of Ancestor Are You Going to Be?

What colors will be added to the Tapestry of Sankofa?
What secret shadows will rest on shoulders sore yet, sentimental?
What words will faithfully follow you into frozen forgotten corners of Time?
What smiles will sing deep down into your Destiny's DNA?
What blueprints will you sew in your grandmother's quilts?
Will stardust fall on your head with icy white whispers
Disguised as Winter Wisdom?
Whose tree will feed you fresh flawless fruit of the future?
What poems will be shift-shaped into bones for you
To stand tall on sadden shoulders.
What daydreams coded into seeds will be planted
On shores of the enslaved, drunk with death?
Whose children will be knighted Young Gifted and Black?
What stone in the river knows how thirsty the hill is?
Whose words will you speak when you meet them?
They are waiting for us.
They are welcoming us.
They are singing our names.
Asking
What kind of Ancestor Are You Going to Be?

Sitting in an Empty Parking Lot

Sitting in an empty parking lot
Under a lamp post dimly lit,
Listening to Jazz quietly humming in my ears.
As...my...fingers feverously find the places
Where your magic spell unlocks the most
Hidden memories of your touch.
Touching...yourtouching...mytouching.
This Black Magic ritual reveals the only
Hidden true treasures where all secrets,
All truths, All sacred joys are sensuously celebrated.
As my long, deep slender messengers send shock waves
Through the bottom of my endless pit of desires.
My fingers play me like the rhythms of a slow sax solo.
Echoing surrounding me, filling me.
My heart beats, the quickening...is near.
My breath is fast. I pant with familiar pleasure.
Eyes closed. Rocking & Swaying. Soon. Hmmmming.
Real Soon Jealous Voyeur.
Mouth Wet with Wild Wonder.
Yes. Oh, Yes.
My fingers fondly fuck me.
They travel like beacons in the fog.
They slip & slide in search of sensuous dessert.
As I sit in an empty parking lot under a lamp post dimly lit.

Juneteenth Ancestors Are African

Juneteenth was born 3 minutes past midnight
One hot cloudless morning after eighteen sunsets in June.
Place: Galveston, Texas. Year: 1865.
Juneteenth parents, grandparents, and great-grandparents
Lived to be over 400 years old.
They hang from Poplar trees all over the South.
Scarred with warm memories & cold realities.
She has daydreams & nightmares at the same time.
She chases sunbeams of justice & slippery shadows of freedom.

Juneteenth, onyx oxymoron.
Mysterious & Misunderstood. Water
Creating a world *from* broken promises.
Surviving a world *of broken* promises.
She walks in secondhand shoes, too tight to feel safe.
She speaks lost languages and Afro Futures.
She studies secrets in shooting stars.
Her African Ancestors are as real as the nose on my face.
She lives covertly in-between the pages of forgotten history.

Juneteenth, the first African American Federal Holiday.
Born from slavery directly into Jim Crow.
Enforcing the echoes of Emancipation.
Enforcing the echoes of Emancipation.
Freeing all Enslaved People forever.
Ending so called "legal slavery."

So, when you hear the name Juneteenth,
Remember to listen with your third eye.
Listen with your first heart.
The ancestors are listening.
They know who & what you are, Juneteenth.
History knows your stories.
Ancestors know your truth.
Slaves did not come from Africa.
Oh no, slaves did not come from Africa.
Teachers, Poets, Healers, Farmers, Architects, Philosophers,

Mathematicians, Scientists, Artists, Inventors, Men, Women, Children, Human Beings
Came from Africa.

My North Star

Miles and miles of melanin midnight sky
Yesterdays' nights daydream about her.
Queen of the Mid-Morning Star
Nine nights, Ninety-nine million steps nearer to North.
And her Naked Negro Shade.
Orion's nighttime lover.
Lonely. Lamentingly longs for Freedom.
Remembering their secrets…
Remembering their resilience…
Remembering…
Ten Thousand whispers
Each effortlessly echoing
Frederick Douglass's wise winter words
Wet with the blood ink of Liberation.

They fly below the storm.
Ten Thousand side-eye slants
Saw Harriet secretly slip into silence.
Quilts on trees, Quilts on fences.
Sing songs to the North Star
On the back of a summer breeze.
Hundreds of hidden less words hiding in plain sight.
See through history's carefully cataract care less eyes.

Sunday's sunset slides in after supper
Hiding crystal cache clouds in the full moon sky
Time. Time.
Time to Travel.
Down Deep on the Road Underground.
One Way along the North Star's Cosmic Highway
"You don't need no ticket; you just get on board."
Ancestral footprints fill your shoes with love and night vision.

Remembering. Remembering.
Human Heroes.

Dead & Alive.
So, steal "A" way.
Steal "Any" way.
Steal Anyway
Home.

Enid Pickett, poet, playwright, teacher, and Healdsburg Jazz Poet Laureate. She has performed with Marcus Shelby, Destiny Muhammad, John Santos, Victor Lewis, and many other artists, at the San Francisco Jazz Center. Enid enjoys sharing her poetry with Abiodun Oyewole of the Last Poets Open House Poetry Gatherings. She has over 30 years teaching experience in both public and private education. Her training includes NEA National Education Association in the Human and Civil Rights Department as a Diversity Trainer as well as an Advisory Board Member for the Southern Poverty Law Center magazine Learning for Justice.

Enid performed at the 75th Anniversary of the United Nations Universal Declaration of Human Rights December 2023. Living in Sonoma County, California Enid served as a Commissioner on the Status of Women and is a co-founder of the Nubian Café Collective, an Edutainment Black Women's Collective. Mother, Fairy Godmother and advocate for human and civil rights. Enid.Pickett.com.

Agu, Prince Osinayah - happyprince

DUCKING GODS.

Fart away,
Fart away, O' mortal,
We were there,
When here was there,
We never left,
To right or to left,
We stood here, where we should,
Your company in bad or good,
From the dawn of you,
Till your certain dusk,
We will claim prized place,
Like The Sacred Tusk,
But, blinded by dark hatred,
Your eyes will not catch a view of us,
For we are in you,
You are in us,
We are you,
You are us,
You are your "ducking" gods.

THE BRIDE

Sound the Ikoro
Flutist, play the finest tunes
Maidens, guide your waists to the rhythm of drumbeats
Wrestlers, fill the ground with your strength

Come from your wretched huts
Come in your wretched clothes
Come with ulcered stomachs
Come prostrating palms

Our god has found his way home
Away from affairs of state
Our voice in the Trinity
Has come again for his bride

Yesterday, we could not shake his hands
Today we will wrap him with hugs and kisses
We will share a meal and pour palm wine from the same keg
But he will wash himself in bleach after the owl had slept

Two hours to the registry
Four hours of scotching sun
A few tubers for bribe
The dowry for a bride

Two hours on a bumpy road
Still draped in organic clothes
Throwing dust in our eyes
Tracing cracks on our feet
Tomorrow, he shall come again riding on German chariots
He will stand behind a wall of Kalashnikovs and wave handshakes at us
We will be his lepers, the quarantined audience at his show
He will steal the bride and rape our ears.

A SONG TO THE DEAD.

Wake up!
Turn your eyes to the sun
Call a yawn from the locker
Raise tired limbs to labour
Rip! Rip! This bubble of conjured reality

Wake up!
A toil is knocking on your palms
On maps that face you
A pendulum of doubts
Divine it!

A log of you is how they pray
A glimpse of you to everyday
To wake is to be seen
To wake is to be sin
Dance on!

A call from you is a ding in the dark
But, how does it hold you from here
Like sleep from season
How did we learn to fear you
Don't stop!
Wake up!
Grasses have sown placentas
Your name is bleeding from the stone
Their ferrous heart is a lie
Or how could they hang you to dry.

AMNESIA

There are days you wake up and forget
The lines you drew on the wall
To retire amnesia from your toil
You rehearsed the moment
Every bit was intact
The words would drop from your lips
Just after night births a new day

It would fall on ears and lips would part
Leaving puckered cheeks
Hands would notice
Limbs would race supine frame to a stump
Day would grow beauty without a sun
Another jubilee of that deportation

A lawn of expectation licked by a cruel fire
Lit by amnesia
Let it sink in like words on knife edge
Blow in windy floods
To caress the bark of doubt

Seething liquor in hollow kangaroo bowl
The substance is more poison
Than the jagged stabs of silence
Of closed doors
And soured goodbyes

This dream is not yours
Didn't fall from your eyes
Like stalls, thrifts, and rifts
Or a peck on the skin of worry

Your visions were here
Clear as bubbles in beer
A warm kiss for a cold night
Was all the mop on due plight

Hold your hands and pray
Raise your feet from clay
Applause over your head
Or bent knees in stead
Away amnesia, away.

ULCERED WALLS
A dead world has no cells to make
It crouches and bows to the plague
Of cornered bites
On tenured plights

The sun is a performer at the circus
A distraction for the genius
Of deaf muses
Drooling artless juices

Come from uphill
A wonder still
The sun is a filter
A troubled soul's shelter.

BE HAPPY
When Sorrow calls, don't answer
When it opens succulent thighs, don't enter
It will drown your soul like a river
And claw your heart like The Reaper

Don't sit where it left you
Don't stand either, it's not your rescue
Hold the hands of Love
And Peace will cover you like a glove.

GOVERNMENT HOUSE

Pity the sun
Pity the moon
Buy the stars some tasty snack
Their lenses have seen worse evil than your eyes

I hear a crack in the court room
A song of breaking bones
Gavel's weight has turned thug
And has torn the Judge's arm from his shoulder

See the roof how it bends on the lintel
Thatched corrugated sins
Held on truss by thick lies
Under the overpriced sculpture of a saint

Excellence has died here
Mediocrity has flowered
Watered by eerie whispers
Trapped ghosts of good intentions

Victims come here but only in prayers
Villains prostrate murderous hands for a pat
Duty done for our collective scorn
Pity us for our eyes have seen evil

Don't let your worries through that gate
It will sire a community in seconds
Let the criminal through to the confessional
Our priest waits with a smile between benevolent arms

The poor must learn to cry in their bones
And wipe their tears with golden handshakes
That palm must never know the charity of water
So, frame it and hang on the wall – your heirloom of a fall

Bastards!
Those AKs tore dreams sore
Those daggers shattered bonds
A smile for a whip will keep this pilgrimage going for a while.

REPROBATES

They comfort the dead
But, mourn the living
They sew patches on heaven
But, hell is bleeding
They dance to the song
On the grave of the gong
They curse tomorrow
With the blessings of today.

OCCUPATION

A note in my hand
Or bullets in your chest
An open robbery in the street
'Thief', rank in the mess

Blind law leading blind justice to the noose
Variegated green, miles away from the war
Sticking bayonets in civilians
Clothed combatants in his eyes

Curdy hair is rapist
Haircut in public.
Law sanctioned exorcisms of loud slaps and hard kicks
Pieces of broken men mass at the *clappery*.

happyprince (Official name: Agu, Prince Osinayah) is a Nigerian experimental poet, performer, and activist. In 2017, he founded the [Aba Poetry Club](), a community of young creatives bound by the belief art is a tool for social change, realizing the Aba Literary Festival in 2019 with a sequel in 2024. He holds a bachelor's degree in Biochemistry from the University of Nigeria Nsukka (UNN) (2011).

He is the Creative Director of Musings of A Madman Art Theatre, a theatre production company which produces his annual solo performance poetry show, Musings of A Madman. The show debuted in 2021 and has had three runs.

He is a prolific believer in the unity of Nigeria and in its boundless implications for the greatness of Africa. He has worked as programme manager at the International Institute for Creative Development, Abuja, (IICDCenter), and Secure D Future International Initiative (SDF) where he works in Grants and Investment, among other roles. He currently works as an art and creative consultant.

happyprince is happily married to Mrs. Agu, Chinyere Judith.

VERNON C. ROBINSON (VCR)
...AND THE LAST SHALL BE FIRST
(a tribute to Abiodun Oyewole of The Last Poets)

A true Bengal tiger
Born in Cincinnati
Earned stripes early
Verbal growls heard in the Empire State
New York, the Big Apple
Poetic consumption down to its core
The birth of Last Poets
On El Haaj's anniversary
And "Emancipation" was not on the menu
For Harlem ears to absorb
So the question of the day...
"What is your thing?"
Question number two...
"Are you ready, Black people?"
Soundtrack of a revolution
Before the Yoruba Society in North Caka-Laka
Baba Dun
One of many birthstones to Hip Hop
Check the DNA
His legacy is ageless
Where hourglasses cheat
And flips upside-down before each final drop of sand
Reach its mountain
I truly understand that time ain't running out
But things are CHANGING
And the time has come
Let Afros and Dashikis be authentic
And not as a trendy novelty
Especially when the revolution comes
While some may party and BS
Party and BS
I'll be building foundations for my community
Printing receipts for my spoken word
Baba Dun
The bop gun to every Sir Nose D'Voidoffunk
The vaccination for the niggeronavirus

Produced by the United Snakes of AmeriKKKa
Evidence that AmeriKKKa IS a terrorist
The power of every verse
Got microphones startling
Transporting messages to nervous speakers
With no choice but to unleash the truth
Baba Dun
The blueprint for Common's corner
The growth for Black roses
Sweet, thornless, eternal
Djembe pounding like raindrops
Blossoming younger plants of culture
To flourish and carry on tradition
And when his transition takes place
When the ancestors receive his poetry
The "Wall Street Journal" will not be capitalized
Honor and respect that man
Hip Hoppers
Respect that man
Today's poets
Respect that man
Elders
Respect that man
Salute to Umar
And Babatunde
And Daveed
And Felipe
And Gylan
And Jalal
And Suliaman
And Nilaja
And Abiodun
Baba Dun
Baba Dun
Recite his pledge forever
To know that we are indeed BLESSED!

CLASS IN SESSION

In the chair I sit
Twiddling thumbs in bewilderment
Classroom full of paralyzed minds
Starving for truth
Teacher feeds rancid history to the brain
Deposit filthy cash into memory bank
Kept in the savings of the lost
Until we become adults
And make a withdrawal of lies
She skipped the chapter
Of us being regal
Went straight to the times
Where we usta labor in cotton fields
And satisfy whiteness in servitude
Our women as sex machines
Our men as human cockfighters
To the death
She talks of Washington, Jefferson, Lincoln
Columbus and those Pilgrims
Taught us how savage and illiterate
The indigenous people were
Martin and Rosa the only folks learnt
That looks like us
Never brought up accomplishments
And world changes produced by our peops
Traffic lights and Almanac and gas masks
And folding cabinet beds and open heart surgeries
And clothes dryers and lawnmowers
And records of several lynchings
And doctors and scientists and entrepreneurs
And revolutionaries and prophets and activists
And composers and athletes
Social studies just a bottle of Nyquil
That keeps us drowsy mentally and intellectually
I bang beats on desks to keep me active
Teacher call it noise
We call it African drums
Inviting the ancestors to maintain our sanity

From the uneducated lessons Monday thru Friday
Black history's been handicapped with
Groundhogs, Presidential celebrations
Super Bowls and heart-shaped goodies
Not to mention a week-long break
To the principal office we go
Sending us back home could be the best decision
Perhaps our village could develop a structure
Where we as a people can know about
Our people
To acknowledge our people
To love our people

MILK CARTON

When lazy bones prohibit heavy chores
But active enough to set sail towards a continent
And snatch up thousands
Who never volunteered to be employed
When enormous ships become aquatic penitentiaries
With no trial or toilets
When Negroes For Labor
Or the original NFL
Are draft picks on auction blocks
Destined to be sold (I mean traded)
To another plantation (I mean franchise)
By a new slave master (I mean general manager)
Where beautiful queens used for breeding
And toxic pleasure
When ropes are designed for dangling bodies
And hatchets for amputations
And that important question asked
What's missing from this equation?
When jealousy destroys Black businesses
And hatred annihilate residents as well
When the experiment in Tuskegee failed tremendously
With syphilis running widespread
When Jim Crow laws produce inferiority
As brown faces are being sautéed with saliva and condiments
At a sit-in lunch counter
While ropes are still dangling bodies back and forth
And we asked again…what's missing from this equation?
When a 14-year old prince sits on a high voltage throne
Accused of murdering two…precious…snow…bunnies
When a mere harmless whistle can lead to
Escorted pickup truck, cotton gin fan and a pistol
Dislodged eye, bullet-holed ear
And a decomposed body floating in the river
Where mama presented an open casket
For the entire world to see
Where the guilty party are set free
Thanks to a soda pop drinking jury
When sticks of dynamite planted like flowers

Except the bloom becomes a BOOM
Exploding that Bama church
Exterminating four young angels off the planet
While ropes are still swinging bodies like pendulums
What's missing from this equation?
When assassinations of Black people are unsolved
Where it's cool to stab a man with a flagpole
Containing stars and stripes
Where a sista's been wrongly convicted in Jersey
With the ugliest mistreatment while imprisoned
In which freedom granted her a one-way ticket to Havana
Yet still enlisted
as the government's public enemy number one
When Boston brothaz are caught in a racial raid by five-o
After a white guy killed his white wife
and enlarged his little white lie
When multiple billy clubs clobbering a motorist on video
Which leads to a riot and bedlum
And ropes are still hoisting bodies like anchors
So what's missing from this equation?
When five young innocent teenagers
can be easily transformed into
Five disgusting animalistic thugs by the powers-that-be
When many are being pulled over on highways and streets
With flashlights blinding eyeballs
And holster to the hip heating up just in case
The suspicious makes any slight movement
When wallets, toy guns and bags of Skittles are lethal
When no-knocks are in full effect
When it's OK to insert bullets to the vertebrae
When it's absolutely fine to apply choke holds
And ignore the plead of one that cannot respire
Meanwhile, those same ropes now drugging bodies
Like "just married" soup cans behind a vehicle
Once again...what's missing from this equation?
Amber alerts contain very little melanin
None of our ebony princesses are named JonBenet Ramsey
Our daughters doesn't possess Natalie Holloway privileges
Living Black men are irrelevant to Black Lives Matter

Until those same men are fatally taken out by pigs
Oh NOW they matter
The media's known to dig up dirt of our victims
Instead of having concern and feeling remorseful
And giving a benefit of a doubt
Instead of automatically determining a guilty verdict
before any evidence
Just 'cause the skin is of mahogany
And the answer to the question
"What's missing from the equation?":
J to the U to the S to the T to the I to the C to the E
And there's no peace without it
There's no rest or relief without it
And time after time we get the dookie end of the stick
Where the tears continue to drench
And the anger continues to build with zero happy endings
Basically we are receiving so-called justice
Simply JUST ICE
With nothing in that glass to quench our thirst
As AmeriKKKA dehydrates our soul over and over
And oh…ropes are still hangin' in there

WANDERIN' IN HEAVEN

Though the past is left behind
I still tend to reminisce
Ran into Sugarfoot from Dayton
Told him "you're right...heaven MUST be like this!"
My aunt was knitting with Dr. Frances Cress Welsing
And then saw Zindziswa Mandela
Reunited with parents Winnie and Nelson
Aaliyah sang while leaning on Duke Ellington's piano
Herman Cain was caught watching Fox News
Then turned the channel
Jim Kelly's teaching my brothers
And Oscar Grant some Kung Fu
Michelle Thomas winks at me
And Fats Waller's like "Hey cat...she's likes you!"
So many children having lots of fun
Saw Tamir Rice and Emmett Till on the X-Box One
Gigi Bryant felt like a child in Disneyworld
Playing double-dutch with those four Birmingham girls
Meanwhile her father Kobe had a one-on-one against Wilt
Gary Coleman try to intervene with a pair of stilts
Miss Hyman giggled and said get off the court
Then he responded "whatchoo talkin' 'bout, Phyllis?"
And then I heard a loud voice
"BIGGIE SMALLS IS THE ILLEST!!"
He was standing between Nat Turner and Eddie Kendricks
And Phife Dawg was enjoying guitar riffs
With Prince and Jimi Hendrix
Such a blessing to see Ruby Dee
Holding hands with Ossie Davis
And Pops Staples ask me once I arrived
How's his daughter Mavis
Phillis Wheatley shared poems
With Amiri, Gil and Maya
And Tammi Terrell loved it when Rick and Teena
Started singing "Fire And Desire"
"Wait...they allow white people in heaven?" I asked
Then Paul Robeson replied

"It's fine…she's the only one who gets a pass."
I've witness Dr. King in a chess game against Malcolm X
And ODB yelled out "YO…I got next!!"
Dr. Sebi continued his diet plan
with Left Eye and Nipsey Hussle
Who was doing a freestyle
with none other than Nipsey Russell
Whitney Houston and Billie Holiday
Sang "Focus" by H.E.R. with Minnie Riperton
And Isabel Sanford hates it
When I call her Weezy Jefferson
Further down was Marcus Garvey building with Dr. Ben
And Bernie Mac had Moms Mabely laughing again
Donny Hathaway serenading Vesta and Lena
Saw Breonna Taylor rollerblading with Bobbi Kristina
James Brown and Roger Troutman produced a new album
for Sean Price
Dorothy Dandridge gave me hug just because she was so nice
Harriet Tubman embraced Sandra Bland
and Trayvon Martin
Said if she was near those cops and Zimmerman
She would've shot them
Michael Jackson greeted me with an upside-down frown
Saying that I no longer have to deal
with that orange-face clown
I saw my dear parents having dinner for two
My friend Michaelle walked over like
"That's gonna be me and you."
Flo-Joy was sprinting while Pac was on the mic
Maurice White played that Kalimba that everyone likes
Sam Cooke did a lovely duet with Betty Wright
And Bessie Coleman gave the Queen of Soul a heavenly flight
"I wanna portray you in a film!"
Says Chadwick Boseman to Medgar Evers
As Fred Hampton crossed his arms and screamed
WAKANDA FOREVER!!

VCR (Vernon C. Robinson) is a Dorchester native born and raised in Boston. He has been writing, reciting and performing poetry/spoken word for two decades, not to mention that he's been emceeing (rapping) for over 30 years. As a poet, VCR has performed at several local open mic spots and gathering as a feature and participant. Venues include Afrocentrics, the Lizard Lounge in Cambridge, The Milky Way Lounge, Ogunnaike Galleria, Strand Theatre, Dudley Café, Haley House and more. He has poetically graced the same stage and opened up for such acts as Dead Prez, S.O.S. Band, Amiri Baraka, Pharoahe Monch, Suheir Hammad, Saul Williams, Lakeside, New Birth, Last Poets, Les Nubians, Jessica Care Moore, Georgia ME, Michel'le and other well-known artists. Besides the Boston and Cambridge areas, he has taken his poetry at cities and states such as New York (including the famous Nuyorican Poets Café), Atlanta, Chicago, Connecticut, Rhode Island, Dallas, Cleveland, New Hampshire, Baltimore, Oakland, Los Angeles, Denver and surprisingly Cuba where he met the legendary Assata Shakur. In 2015, he was an opening act for the ArtsEmerson musical/play "Breath & Imagination" in Boston.

VCR is also a cultural event organizer under the company known as BloodSkinLand Productions. From that umbrella, he has created many annual gatherings which include Winter Words, Maylennium, Devotion...Black Love Day, Megacipher, SistaHood, Body Language, BomBARDed, Afro-Cinema, Young Gifted & Black, InFRESHstructure and The Red Black & Green Affair (a dedication to Marcus Garvey). His most recognized gathering is an ongoing event called VerBaLizAtiOn which is currently the longest-running open mic spot in the Boston area of over 25 years.

Through VCR's performances, there is an array of memorable poems that are popular to the ears of spectators who have witnessed his stage presence whenever blessed the microphone. Poems such as ***"Tooth Decay"*** and ***"Alphabet Killaz"*** are among the favorite from supporters of VCR's work. In fact, those two pieces and others can be found on the debut CD of VCR entitled *"Poetic Insanity"*. VCR has been nominated for Best Male Spoken Word Artist at the 2006 New England Urban Music Awards and twice for Best Spoken Word Artist at the 2006 & 2007 M.I.C. Hip-Hop Awards. In 2011, he became an recipient of the NAACP Image Awards of the Boston chapter. In 2014 he was awarded the Ralph F. Browne Jr. Juneteenth Incentive Award for his continuous work through VerBaLizAtiOn. VCR's "Kangaroo Joy" became the official poem for then Boston City Councilor At-Large and current Massachusetts Congresswoman Ayanna Pressley's annually "Jump Into Peace" event. In addition to that, he has also performed at the Congresswoman's cultural arts swearing-in fundraiser with a poem entitled *"Change Can't Wait"* – named after the slogan used by Pressley during her campaign.

VERNON C. ROBINSON (VCR)
bloodskinland@yahoo.com
(617) 480-7663

Ishmael Street

Purple Heart

Sometimes gunfire shines
better than sun.
Heaven smile like burning
flesh.
I left the war, but the war didn't
leave me.
Causing chaos in my mind
and heart.

I can't murder these memories,
they are part of me.
Death is my only true
redemption.
No one can save me.
cleanse me.

I'm not a hero, I'm humanity's
villain.
These scars of war will never heal.
My only redemption is holding
a bible in my left hand and
a gun as I slowly
rasise it to my temple.
I see the lives I have a taken
from the fog of war staring
at me.
No one speaks and I feel
they eagerly awaiting for me to
pull the trigger.
I don't hesitate, pull the trigger
like a cello
The sound of fireworks piercing
my flesh.
My soul is crying because life has my body.
For I'm forever causality of war.

History

I don't want to be a extension
of your history
Nor your colonized folklore.
Don't put my story in your
books or songs
I'm not American Dream
I'm Ancestors Dream
You will not appropriate me
like MLK or Mandela
Nor based on true story of me
You will not find my story in
a Walmart Target or fucking
Dollar tree.
I'm Ancestors Dream
Not American Dream
I'm before Columbus
I'm the Haitian Revolution
I'm the first African president of the America's
VINCENTE Guerrero
You will not Tulsa me or Ocoee
me.
You will not gentrify my story
Cause this is my story
And I'll tell my own fucking story!!!

———

Ishmael Street started as a Marketing Director, a Publicity and Talent Relations Director for two radio shows (The Lovejones Experience With Goddess Jones and Hip Hop Today/Red Cup Radio), which he interviewed guests like comedian legend Michael Coylar, filmmakers Erica Watson, and much more. Ishmael was a Marketing Director of hip-hop's literary series called The Chronicles Of A Hip Hop Legend which became the Chronicles Of A Hip Hop Legend Radio Show where he co-produced the show having legends like Speech from Arrested Development, MC Shan, Raposdy, Camp Lo, and more. Now, he is the founder, creator, producer, and host of the Dad Is Not A Noun Podcast available on YouTube and All Audio Platforms and Marketing Consultant for the non-profit organization Real Dads Network.

Elemen2al
I'm So Dope...

I been dope
Since conception,
Grown from
Poppy seed
& Mama's gardening—
Where phases turned sonnets
Become smack-soaked serotoni.

There is no spoon

Pure enough to smoke,
Blue Magic
In a revolutionary's body

Talkin' that
Black righteous space shyt,
Outkasted
By flicks of pens
Deep as nautilus.

These jellyfish-infested stanzas
Make plankton question—
Quaalude inducted coordinates
In leagues of killer beings.

Make it bubble (chemical).
Call it Aqualung.
Another QP
Hydroponic (16),
MDMAmbien (metaphor's dream).

They'll love me
In mornings after—
Just a bump
To get over that
Hump day
& fly yo high ass to paydays

So American Gangsta,
Slanging metric tons of
Pfizer Frank White truth,
Recycled, repackaged, & repurposed
As extremist.

Malcolm Little's
Last fix,
The X in Pandora's boxes.

I'm so dope,
I cardiac arrest—
CPR respiratory repetition,
Squeezing life back into lungs
While stealing it
From the living

Sativa believer,
Chase dragons
From opium dens.
Scorpion pen,
Kin to shark's fin—Overdose flow

I murdered a rock,
Injured every rolling stone
Not named temptations,
Hospitalized a brick.

I'm so dope
I make antidotes sick.

So oxy,
I'm Xanny – nose candy,
Soft as cyanide's kiss
With methadone methods.

Think Heisenberg,
Klonopin tails on chemtrails.

I been hailed – the most addictive.

I'm so dope—
Oxytocin potency,
Spit dopamine.
I mean,
      I'm dope.
           I mean,
      I'm Dope.
I mean,
Fresh off
The fentanyl patch
With a reckless, restless tongue—
Call it plug talk.

Don't ever think
You can throw words
At wizards
Who bleed morphine,
      Sweat coca leaves,
           And dream in CC's of alchemy.

I'm so dope wit it,
I give the hopeless
A fearless voice
That's just as dope
As the ancestors hoped.

Whitey on the Throne

Recently
We saw a system
Work as designed—
Priming pumps
To get this
Grand Ole Opry
Back in order

To rewrite coordinates
From iceberg & slim pickens
To its glorious Titanic
Intentions.

Back
To Days of Thunder—
Burning rubber,
Petty, Intimidator style.
Call it
Wonder Bread miracle whips.
No Ricky Bobby.

This reality—
I mean TV—
I mean dramaturgy
Flexing chops
On stages larger than life
Under red & blue skylines.

Keep bloodlines secure
As 4th & Goal,
Where wins become losses—
Call it witching hour.

Whole country
In Red Zone panic,

Or sleeping soundly snug as snub nose,
Maybe Primrose
In District 13.

Now that
Whitey's on the throne,
Since swing states swung
& home run election numbers—
War has come to suburbia,

Where all is fair
When you hang with guerillas
Draped in red hats—
Make new Axis,
Checkered flag.

Call it 9-1-1,
Cause Whitey's on the throne.

Even though
Whitey's on the Moon
With designer spacesuits,
Riding privilege rockets
From Village to Metropolis—
With lowercase g
Gold-like purse strings,

Made weapons of greed,
Where schemes become thieves—
To enrich lives
Or define divine providence.

That Big E everything
Is their birthright.

Dollars to donuts,
No J Dilla.

Just diligently
Paying homage
To Caesar's holy ghost of
Heroes through hostages

How quickly savagery
Became slavery
In textbooks—
Turned rest haven for
Every Reich outta step,
Tryna keep up with

Jones',Combs' (Maybe not Combs'),
Sherlock Holmes could see—
Elementary, My dear Edison—Tesla,

@ Amazon market value of Capitol,
On Capitol steps of imperialism

Call it
      Disney,
           Walton,
                Bezos,
    Or Ellison.

Musk must be
Praising almighty dollars,
Holla hallelujah gold standard—
With Whitey on the throne.
See how this
American Gangster's bank account
So Super PAC'd

With good-clean-
....OLD money—
That COAL money,
....That OIL money,

Now that Whitey's on the throne.

Call it privilege,
Or $ million loan
From Daddy Warbucks—
In slumlords we trust,

Connoisseurs of disgusting.
Now—His son is sun
For those clamoring
In despot darkness called
Once upon a time

That suddenly sounds like
45 became 47—
On track turned office,
Where rubbing is racing to
Top of food chains

Maybe Oppenheimer Barbie codes,
Or NASCAR point standings—
To masquerade their malevolence
Into macabre matrix of Morpheus,

Wrapped in Hypnos,
Called Nosis
Or No sense - or politicsKarening—
....I mean Caroling—
........I mean singing—

Weather outside is frightful,
Filled with rivals or
Bible-thumping revivals,
Where idols conjure
Merry Whiteness

Baring likeness to
A Linus crisis—
I mean America's finest
      Has reminded us:

Their highness
Is finally home

So send this chaos
Priority mail—Special—
Back to Whitey on the throne!

Elemen2al is a poetic force dedicated to truth, justice, and amplifying marginalized voices. From his 2014 debut at Glassless Minds to global recognition, his words resonate on stages like Nuyorican Poets Café and NJPAC. Author of *Calamity* (2021) and featured in impactful anthologies, he blends artistry with activism. A leader behind the scenes and on stage, Elemen2al is more than a poet—he is a catalyst for change. Elemen2al.com

Paul Richmond

How Do I See My Own History

The history of my family origins
Ends with each of my grandparents
Arriving in America
No stories, information was passed on
Except country of origin
One was Poland and the other Russian
That is what was stamped on the passports

Public records can be used to find out
Where I lived
What schools I went to
Who my family members are

I remember all my girlfriends
I don't know if they remember me

As technology has changed
From using a pay phone
That kept my identity a secret

My present phone
Locates me where I am
Keeps a record of who I called
What pictures I have taken
Who I have communicated with
How I think and what I have said
Who my friends are that I have never met

In the past
Governments spent vast amounts of money and time
To watch people, record their activities, collect the evidence
Showing they are resisting and need to be remove

Now with the devices we are forced to use
We give the governmental corporations all the info they need
Each new technology

Tracks us more efficiently
Occupies more and more of our time

I am told if I go to my account
At the top of the screen
I will see the navigation panel menu
Click security & privacy
Find History in the list
Click History

I see my activities that have been recorded
Which are not private or secure

Here's a picture of the great lunch I had
When I was working

Here's a picture that was posted to my profile
Someone took of themselves
As they were giving me money
Showing everyone, they cared
When I was panhandling for a lunch

When I read about Poland and Russia today
I read about them with a language that doesn't know them
There are foods I eat that I am told came from there
I am an observer of a past I cannot see

I learned in school that my families were among millions
Coming to escape violence and persecution
To the land of the free called United States of America
With that I am told I am an American

America slaughtered the people who were living here
America brought people here and made them slaves
America built an empire with endless wars
America the Good Guys
In history books written by America

It is said if the lion is the only one writing down the history
We never hear about the pry that got away
Being killed by the water buffalo
The history we are told is the lions are the king of the jungle

Excuse me
My phone is buzzing
I feel the need to look at it
It is showing me an event I did in the past
Saying that my history matters to them
Perhaps I want to share this memory
A way of reliving the past
And invite others to the past with me

I have decided to disregard the buzzing device

Instead,
I focus on the activities in front of me
Knowing
I am creating history

Life

Growing up
There was a magazine called
Life

My mother being the first born here
From Poland
Tried to look like the women
In Life Magazine
To be American
You needed to look White American
She rarely spoke in public
She didn't want you to hear the Polish
She was looking Life magazine White American

Before computers, the internet influencers
A wooden box sat in the corner of the room
A black and White screen would light up
On turning one of the knobs
Our choices were limited to three channels
Magazines were another source of information
Magazines told us what Life was about
How to look
What was cool, sexy and in

Looking back
I saw images of myself there
Which came first
My expression
Or like my mother
I started looking
Like the ones they said were radical
The Freaks
The War protestors
The counterculture

The standards of success
Were shown to us there
Did my life mean anything

Was there a picture of me doing it
In Life Magazine

Life Magazine
Defined by White America
The moving up in the world
What clothes, cars, houses defined your success
When you made it in Life
You were in Life magazine

In Buffalo in the 70's
Living in colored neighborhoods
People took pride in dressing to the T
I was asked why I was throwing away my suit
Looking like I was living on the street

Seeing the death in the clothes, cars and houses
As they were defined
They weren't showing alternative lifestyles
And when they did
Gypsies, Tramps & Thieves were called up
The poor families who lost their kids
To the Hippies

Life magazine
Culture, news, propaganda
Captured in pictures
Marilyn Monroe
The Beatles
Civil Rights Equal Rights demonstrations
The Vietnam war to name a few

Those who profit from wars
Leaned it wasn't such a good idea
To show too many pictures in Life Magazine
Of the bodies piling up
Disfigured faces
Guns pointed at women and children
Seeing life being wasted, destroyed in color
In Life Magazine

To have your face on the cover of Life Magazine
You were somebody
Muhammad Ali fought his way there

The life I chose
Wasn't shown to me in Life magazine
Other magazines came along
Talking about getting back to the land
Leaving a smaller footprint
Thinking sustainable over consumable
Equal and civil rights
A world without war

Occasionally Life magazine
Would do a story about these things
Surrounded by the ads
For the big cars and diamond rings

I was asked
How do I feel about the life I lived
As if my life is over

I said
Stop thrown dirt on me
I am not dead yet

There are regrets
Broken hearts

I spent more time at the beach
Then I did in an office
I spent more time wrapped around lovers
Then buying products to make me feel sexy

I spent more time enjoying each day and moment
Instead of waiting until I was too old
To remember what I enjoyed

Life Magazine died in December of 1972
The reason
It was too expensive to keep it alive

1972 my adult life was beginning
There were times I wondered
How long it would continue
I now wonder if it will become too expensive

Life Magazine came back a few times
In different forms
We all need to adapt and change course
If we hope to stay in the game

In the end
When we get the call
When you really love life
There is no regret or anger
Just a sadness
Of too bad
I am having a good time
I wish it could go on for a little longer

Music

When I was 10 years old
For a birthday present
I was given a rocket

It wasn't really a rocket
It had two wires with two clips
That you attached to the radiator
There was a plug for earphones
The top of the rocket
Had a round ball that when you pulled it up
It was attached to a metal rod
As you made it smaller and larger
You heard voices
You heard music
It was my first radio
I could listen to anything I wanted
At any time
It brought other worlds into my dark bedroom

Riding in cars
The radio
Played what was popular
I learned what I was supposed to listen to

When I was older
I saved my money and bought my first stereo
It was a box with the turn table and speakers all together
It was cheaper than the individual parts
I could play what I wanted, when I wanted
Listen to it over and over, in my bedroom

I discover underground record shops
Not the ones in the malls
These were in basements
With bins and bins of records
Where you were influenced by the covers
Not knowing what the music was like inside
It is when your status was based on your record collection

Or if you were the one everyone went to
To find out about the next new music to listen to

Then there were the live concerts
My first was at a venue my parent's generation saw shows
We were forced to wear suits and ties
It was that kind of place
The suits and ties were taken off
In my friend's older sister's car
Who took us to the show
It was The Who
Who smashed their instruments
And went wild
Taking off the suits and ties was just the beginning

Being at the Filmore East in NYC
For the midnight to dawn shows
Was another initiation into the hip
Then there was Woodstock
Tickets were bought for $12 for the weekend
We were pulled over by the police several times
Made it off the exit before it was shut down
Leaving the car in the fields with the others
Walking and riding on cars until we got to the site
Where all the fences were taken down
We didn't need our tickets

We were given the illusion that we had great numbers
Where all the rallying cries that we sang daily
Were all together
The finger was given to the system
The police stood around helpless
Watched us smoke pot, share, sell LSD
We outnumbered them

The songs were sung without the words being censored
As they had been on the radio or on the juke boxes

Fuck you and we are the revolution
This was mostly for white kids

The cities, suburbs, schools
And spaces for cultural integration
Were largely segregated at that time

15% of the 150 artists
Who performed at Woodstock
Were artists of color
The music played was influenced by African American music
Richie Havens captured the crowd
African American music despite the segregation
Had white fans
The "heroes" started dying
Along with all the assassinations
Fellow students being killed on campus
The song 4 dead in Ohio became one of the anthems

Then the punks spit on peace and love
Since they were being kicked in the head
The music was louder and harsher
The dancing a public friendly brawl
Singing "There is no future, There is no future"

After the police and national guard killings
Being arrested for my values
I went back to the land
No stereos, concerts, no radio
The land, where the trees sing

New technologies multiplied the choices
Hearing music from everywhere by everyone
Learning about all this music
That had come and gone
While I was listening to the trees

Now concerts are hundreds to thousands of dollars
The new stars are not the revolution
While most musicians struggle to make ends meet
Music has spoken to humanity
Since the first drum
The cry of a voice

Knowing how important
Hearing a song
That brings hope
Encourages a spirit to carry on
Don't give up

I have joined those on stage
Adding to the choices
To create more than mind numbing white noise

Without being taught
The kindergartners at the free school
Just started dancing when music was put on
These moves are their own
These sounds that they never heard before
Call out for their bodies to move

It is time to start banging on something
Uncage your voice
Scream out to the wild

For the survival of future generations
Create and turn up the Music

Paul Richmond has been a university professor, worked in a worker run warehouse, a professional juggler, writer, performer, organizer, publisher and activist. He was

awarded and named by the National Beat Poetry Foundation a Beat Poet Laureate for MA 2017 - 2019, US Beat Poet Laureate 2019 - 2020 & Lifetime 2022. He has performed solo nationally and internationally. With the ensemble *Do It Now* who showcased at the *Edinburgh Fringe Festival*. Publisher of 80+ Authors. He has 8 books. www,humanerrorpublishing.com

Devynity

Women I Come From

I come from women that never put they bags on the floor
them that would clean they houses on Saturdays
while Soul Train was on
They get in they groove
while they favorite jams play
and sweep and mop and scrub and sway
my type of women

I come from women that burn incense
and wear a lot of of bracelets
You can hear 'em coming from far
Jinglin' baby
women that wear waist beads
And headties
Them ones that lay their heads on satin pillowcases
wake up with a crook in they neck tryna protect
they style
all that money they spent it gotta last
my kinda women

I come from women that smell like oils and sacred fragrances
Women that throw shade and will read you in curt and
abrupt phrases
Them ones that are hard to interrupt
Women that will pull up/ pop shit
Keep secrets and gossip

I come from women
That make the "I'm only eating her potato salad" potato salad
Mac & cheese, baked beans, bread pudding
I come from women that put gravy wit the stuffing
Them ones that make something
Outta nothing/ Then call it lemonade
Them ones that even when they scared to death
Walk up battle-ready, brave

Never looking afraid
My kind of women
Them ones that demand excellence
Them ones that raise and back you
Them ones that if you dare talk back to?
Will haul off and smack you
Won't hesitate to raise a backhand,
throw something at you/ Stab you
I come from women with attitude
Women that wield weapons
In the art of interrogation exhibit the highest aptitude
Them ones that laugh at dudes who fail to come correct
I come from women you don't disrespect

My kinda women
Keep pearls and crystals
Light candles and make tinctures
Burn sage and wipe ash
And always keep a stash
For just in case
I come from women that know how to come and go
and leave no trace

women with eyes in the back of they head
strong in they stride
lioness pride
my kinda women

I come from women that don't leave the house
in their house clothes
Women that won't leave the house with their heads tied
or without their earrings on
Unless they going out to fight
I come from women that put on lotion one limb at a time
Carry some to go in they purse
Women that fight before they cry
If they cry at all
Women that when faced with shitty options, still decide
And ride
Never off into sunsets

But up into clouds and smoke and
Out into waves, they float
Greeting mami wata with their heads bowed
Women that sat me up on phonebooks
to part and grease my hair
To prepare my scalp for that relaxer just to burn all of them
naps outta my kitchen
Women forced to carry heavy loads
even in a delicate condition

I come from women that go down to the basement
and spoon out church dinners
To bring home a couple of plates
Humming in delicious whispers
Saved women, sinners
saviors, killers
I come from women that sit in pews; taking up collections
without the plates
Women that speak their mind, amazing how they grace
My kind of women

THE FORCE

An anthropological study

White people love to police
Inspect
inquire
Poke they head out
Get a look at
Have a look see
Ask a lot of questions
Investigate
Interrogate
All so they all feel safe

Find out what all is going on over there yonder
Cuz if you wasn't there yesterday,
you shouldn't be there tomorruh
Nah
Where you come from?
You can't be from here
White people love to interfere
Interrupt
Intimidate
Equivocate
All so that they all feel safe

White people love to stake a claim
With a rod and a staff
Orate a proclamation
Land on your spot and pitch a flag
Take a drill to your land, dig a ditch in your sand
Mine your gold and with cash in hand
Demand that you move
Numb to the abuse as if it was painless
They'll call it drainage
They drink the milkshake up
Then bring them boys to your yard
Draw lines on they maps where they never were
Invent a boundary

Impose a barrier
Spread a sickness
Be cause and carrier

White people love to insist
Interject
And infringe upon
Always wanna touch & get a feel for it
White people call their massacres manifest destiny
Their extremism supremacy
Their riots insurrection
They call the Civil War the war of northern aggression
Wave a Confederate flag
Pervert the source
Commodifying is all par for the course
They enforce
Then call their force,
The Force

Devynity is a Black woman writer and visual artist from Queens, NY, whose work reflects her heritage and upbringing. Devynity's written and visual work are intertwined, both mediums offering a space to examine contemporary themes within the Black experience to illuminate the nuanced stories of struggle, resilience, love, and trans-formation that shape her communities and the diaspora at large. Her practice explores how race, gender, and history collide and collude to impact personal and collective identity. At the heart of her words is a commitment to truth-telling: honoring the past, engaging with the present and imagining a future grounded in authenticity and empowerment — always in furtherance of a broader dialogue about representation and the ongoing journey towards justice and equity.

Devynity attended NYC's notorious LaGuardia High School of Music, Art & the Performing Arts as an art major. She holds a BA in Africana, Puero-Rican and Latino Studies from CUNY's Hunter College and and MFA in Visual Arts from Lesley University. She was a Grand Slam Finalist and team member at the Nuyorican Poet's Café in 2002 which competed in the National Grand Slam ranking 3rd that year among 53 other teams. Her poem "Black Girl Manifesto" was published in Hill Harper's bestseller Letters to a Young Sister. She continues to perform and exhibit artwork throughout the city and regionally.

Karega Ani

On the Matter of White Lives (Somebody Did…)

In his infinite and infallible wisdom
God
did not
make them
"white"
but somebody did
the specter of Bacon's Rebellion
sizzles in the era betwixt
the crack and opiate epidemics
its lessons missed
in the midst of the myth of differences
and the myriad afflictions
statistically splitting the distance
between the ghetto and tornado alleyways
back in the olden days
there was an aspirational saying
pertaining to the truth making one
free
but in this age of agit-propaganda
accuracy vanishes in echo chambers
and inconvenient histories
disappear from memory
the Great American narrative
is black
and white
and red all over the pavement
a patriotic web of deceptions
fashioned from fabulist velvet barriers
a pairing of champagne wishes
and red herrings
a market interest
obfuscating what ought to be
the obviously comparable scars
of black backs
and rednecks

contrary to gist of all the marching
and the posturing
and arsenals
our common history
got us all sitting in the middle of the crosshairs
it's got us choking
on the gunsmoke wafting through
our local high school auditoriums
and segregated sanctuaries
wheezing and coughing
as the non-fiction bonfires gleam
the sickest characteristic of hell
is that all of its residents have
forgotten that they got the keys
clearly
God
did not
make them
"white"
but somebody did
and ever since then they've been addicted
to the bliss of forgetting
generation after generation
they willfully spread and bend
vigorously getting bleached
from the annals of history
willful ignorance rebranded as an identity
swinging from the branches of their bigotries
feverishly cutting accent
and color from their collective memories
desperately seeking respite
from the distress of ethnicity
but these cannon fodder track stars
can not fathom
the absolute contempt of the gentry
too busy seeking validation
to ever re-evaluate the real enemy
and the existential threat
of their protected
and exalted mediocrity

this zero-sum game calculus
has these feeble minded descendants
of the huddling masses
playing into the hands of their handlers
this zero-sum game calculus
has these Christian nationalist fanatics
descending into madness
gripping flag poles
and ransacking capitals
this zero sum game calculus
has these anti-intellectual manic-depressive
panhandling grandkids
of the potato famine
masquerading as the "master race"
a mad gaggle of passé riché vagrants
collapsing after chasing trinkets
dangling just out of range
and they've been the jackasses
in this sick sad arrangement
ever since back in the day
a vacuous plantation of pack animals
saddled with overdrafted aspirations
unable to see the irony in
chump change slave chasing to stay free
chain slinging as a means to an end
praying they can trade in sable skins
for gilded fleeces
their epigenetic guilt tripping
their collective amygdalas
whenever they see
a nigger living and breathing
see the thing is
God
did not
make them
"white"
but somebody did
and there they kneel
amidst the remnants of their dignity

and grievances
obsequiously seeking
to be visible for once
still believing
they can please "them" just enough
to be considered
something other than
expendable for once
but the die is caste
and asinine allegiances
no matter how vehemently pledged
can not protect them
from the cannibalism
of their masters in the end

this empire
is defended by the ambitions
of sycophants and simpletons
it is defended by
the remnants of resentments
hidden under rusted tongues
and cutting duplicity
it is defended by
the double crosses wrought
from starvation thrown bones
and gourmet table scraps
it is defended by
the grandiose notions grasped
in the hopeful calloused hands
of the deluded underclass
it is defended by
the radio-activists'
sound bombs detonated
in the pleasure centers
of the 2nd amendment apostolic
trailer park avenue romanticists
it is defended by
the black lung cancer bandwagons
of sacrificial assassins

this empire is defended by
the foolish opportunists
doomed by the illusion of inclusion
and the immutable gloominess
of the dawn's early light
God
did not
make them
"white"...
but somebody did
and deep in the recesses of their genetics
they remember
they remember the rebellion
they remember battling the real oppressors
they remember but the fear is
the John Brown prophylactic
the fear is
the perennial tar baby trap
snatching them back into position
the fear is
the DW Griffith pitch black apparition
triggering the visceral reactions of
the grand dragon actors
and the backwater vagabonds
the hound dog tramps
and the slack-jawed alcoholics
the hillbillies
the hicks
the half-witted MAGA rally fanatics
and the easily manipulated simpletons
eagerly defending this system
even if its killing them
and the abyss is getting deeper
by the second
the implications of the grift
splitting the distance between
the present and armageddon
replacing evidence with
with revisionist narratives

resulting in asphyxiated brain dead babies
that never question the validity of any of it
in her infinite and infallible wisdom
God
did not
make them
"white"…
but somebody damn sho' did
ostensibly
there was a time
when they demanded liberty
but in the end
they settled for permission
they settled for the sensationalism
of being considered
"better" than the designated "them"
of the day
and in the wake of the delirium
the devil disappeared
without a trace

War Drum (Standing Battleground)

This is for we the people
kneeling in temples contemplating loaded shotgun
contradictions like
how much does free cost?
Can sovereignty be given or is it always a product of conflict?
Is there such a thing as pacifistic self-defense?
What monsters must we all become to overcome the
monstrous or
what gives us the gall to kill the religions we've been given
and resurrect the God within us?
this is for we the people
boldly questioning in an era of deadly curiosity
panting and running from a rabid pack of wild dogmas
embracing the unending dichotomy of liberty or death

this is for us
the blues people at the 11th hour
of purple majesties and memories
red eyes
and gold minds discarded as tokens
sitting alone in crowded silences
ruminating on the darkness and the miracle of all
that we have been and are becoming
congregating in the shadows of our ancestors
assembling the echoes of the wild
wild narratives from whence we've come
this is for us
the blues people
reawakened and making sorrows into prophecy and power

this is for
the defiant ones
the outliers accepting nothing less than loud and unabashed
truth
knowing that emancipation comes in the embrace of love
and in the fearless recognition that this embrace means war
knowing that the entire planet is a battle ground

and that the need for revolution is as endless as greed is
this is for the defiant ones
rumbling in a battle of attrition
the incessant rebels
rejecting the unacceptable constrictions
living beyond the implicit contradictions
this system has engineered to limit them
to the misfits of gender and border
to the black sheep absent fences apprehension and order
for the defiant ones
determining themselves in the holy name of tomorrow
and becoming all they will
keep fighting
to see the light
keep fighting
to reach the light
keep fighting
to teach the light
keep fighting
to keep the light
keep fighting
to be the light
keep fighting
knowing that life itself
is hanging in the balance

Karega Ani (Awo Ifatunmo Ifayori Fayemi) is a Poet, Priest, Husband, Father, Son, Brother, and multi-hyphenate artist from Houston, TX. He holds a BS in Psychology from Prairie View A&M University and an MA in Social Justice from Marygrove College. He has released two poetry collections, Black Ivory (2016), and My Big Black Audacity (2018). He has also released three full length recording projects, Open (2001), The Eyes of the World (2004), and Concentrated Substance: The Chronicles of a Hopeless Optimist (2011). Ani has also been published in The Pierian Literary Journal (Albany State University), and has graced the pages of numerous other publications over the span of his career. He currently resides in the Greater Atlanta area.

a g

"WE SWAYED"

(Ancestral hums commence, as sounds of the djembe ascends)

WE SWAYED.

from side to side
with each wave
melanated splintered skin--
bodies--
head & tail laid
for maximum room saved
tragically made
into servants
with purpose perverted
a symbiosis of ritualistic delusion & barbaric inclusion
adverse effects through the times
cascade

WE SWAYED.

from the limbs of ambiguity & deciet
to the beat of mindless mob banter
enslaved to the
practiced prattle passed on through the periods
generations fueled by
misplaced hate
engendering exelerated equinoxes of deprecation
actively ignored traces of light

WE SWAYED.

like beautiful bright bulbs
blooming under the sun
dancing in the vertiginous winds
admired
jealously---

from the supported shadows of false Supremacy
plucked from the roots
forcefully immersed in vicissitudes

WE SWAYED.

like patient boxers on a stage
transfering our weight
until the proper opprotunity to engage
you thought we were falling---
really
we are being moved by Spirit
BACK INTO OUR TRUTH
before it was misconstrued
raped...
exploited...
abused...
WE ALWAYS RISE FROM THE INFERNO

(Ancestral hums)

Seeds are eternal.

a g is a passionate Hartford, CT native of Caribbean decent. As a prominent creative and caregiver, they are dedicated to empowering their community by cultivating inclusive spaces for wellness, evolution and self expression. From visual or performance art to auditory compilations, they infuse every creation with authenticity and altruism.

Currently, a g is channeling their energy into building Walk In Veracity LLC, a beautiful business venture that embodies these core principles. In addition, to their artistic pursuits, they serve as an Employment Specialist for a local non-profit, supporting neurodivergent adults in leading independent and meaningful lives.

With divine direction from The Most High, a g is committed to ascension through self exploration, healing and fulfulling their purpose in life.

Baba Ngoma Osayemi Ifatunmise

The Statue of Liberty is Pissed

The statue of liberty is pissed
she's got give me your tired your poor
tattoed at her feet
but originally there were chains around her ankles
they still remain
that's why Trumpleskinthin
has the nerve to say immigrants ruin the country
I guess he cut class
when the truth was told that
we are oppressed nationalities
the world is full of oppressed nationalities
war is profitable
so the dispossessed
still struggle to own their own tomorrow
Ignorance tried to crucify democracy
but she refuses o die
so we're at the dollar store
where everything cost two dollars
wondering how much this balloon of inflation
can stand before it explodes
and I'm thinking about
a world without TV
there are so many starving
displaced from their homes
by the rockets red glare
who never knew what XBOX was like
now the children are
quick on the trigger finger
practicing for never ending war
when their world is demolished
yesterday will never be again
struggling for existence
as we ponder what the future
might be
since a world war seems inevitable

the news makes Revelations
seem like a fairy tale
and everyone is depending on Hope
but Hope is lost
destroyed in Gaza
as professional victims
act like Hitler
the 4th Reich
seems like a house party
and Armaggedon
is much more
than a Bible story waiting for reality
maybe Elijah was right

Show Me What Democracy Looks Like

soon we may see what democracy looks like
up close with it's bloody hands
around your throat
machine gun pointed at your head
the clash of red and blue
splattered purple on the white house wall
as the tourniquet tightens
like a noose
to stop the bleeding of the cost of war
but sometimes karma blows back in your face
like pissing in the wind
as this prophecy falls
like acid rain
deadly as h.i.v.
so you'd better be strapped
and i don't mean your gat
well maybe you'd best bring that too
the teabaggers put a bandage on the gash
but stashed a lot of cash
blocking loot for education, senior centers
and healthcare
racing to pay soldiers
for the wars they have created
as we worry if the luck of the draw
will come up busted in this
lifegame of blackjack
a reality show where nobody knows
just how deep the rabbit hole goes
or if the cord on this bungee
will snap without a safety net
in this deal made with the devil
public enemy already told you
"Can't trust 'em"
now we wait to find
how resistance will be treated in
banneker city
or if the u.n. will have to intervene
like libya on the potomac
show me what democracy looks like

Today is the Tomorrow
We were Looking for Yesterday

Today is the tomorrow
we were looking for yesterday
1984 on roids
behold a pale horse on oxy
this sure aint wonderland Alice
little orphan annie
iives in tent city
underneath the rail yard
down by the tracks
even white folk got problems
poverty is color blind
only on Fox 5
is the economy booming
as vampires suck
blood for oil
and use your children as cannon fodder
war is endless and profitable
and we've started wars on lies before
what makes it different this time
when were we never at war
9/11 was an inside job
why not have a day
when the misleaders call for battle
and everyone stays at home
Tell your children combat is deadly
and perilous to your health
paint protest signs
on the walls of your consciousness
remember
the military is an industrial complex
but it's not too complex to see
the chicken hawks only send our kids
to fight their conquests
do u think a million people rallying
in Baneker City
could snatch the yardbirds
out of the palace

Is there a law
that would make actually
make them read the constitution
This is the state of emergency
poets told you about
I would continue with this catastrophe
but it's just too much to twitter

Seeds

All the new is bad
I've started to watch sports
I'm a musician
I don't give a damn about sports
so this is raising havoc
on my equilibrium
I have issues cause
there is no down beat
and the bands play racist sexist music
rotation on the radio is mostly garbage
Real Hip Hop was poisoned a long time ago
and I'm praying for some new organic crop
but the only thing I get is
regurgitated garbage
Beyonce's trying to bring Country back
it's been stolen with Bluegrass
along with peace and justice
It's all African anyway
Oh, I forgot
we're still searching for peace and justice
It's been gone much longer than
bebop and hip hop
I need my drum rhythms back
matter of fact but that's another thesis
the ancestors said
"they tried to bury us.they didn't know
we were seeds
the problem is that the ground is barren
worn out from crop rotation
but there's still plenty of compost
the roots of african rhythm still prevail
Viva Fela reincarnate
the seeds of rhythm reign
and we plant them wherever we go

Look The Theory of Everything

They want you to believe it was Eve

but it wasn't her

the Greeks act like it's Lilith

but a skull found on a mountain top

in Kenya

was knicknamed Lucy

cause Lucy in the Sky with Diamonds

was playing

when she was discovered

they try to say they discovered everything

but heart beats like drum beats never lie

at least not to us

we summoned gods with polyrhythm

that's why they took our wawa coh away

we did the two step

before culture bandits waltzed

or walked upright for that matter

it's said they crawled in caves

where the light never shined

while our 3rd eyes drank melanin

from the Sun Son

architects built pyramids

and hid the secrets

as we wailed pentatonic scales

on full moon nights

making ebb tides flow

they couldn't understand the science

nor the math of Yidaki vibrations

primordial sounds of trance

dreaming the universe into being

long before Alkebulan broke off

floating down under to be misnamed Australia

when the beauty of nakedness became a sin

They try to say they discovered everything

our bare feet hoofed beats before shoes

when they took our drums

our slave songs signaled Tubman

to help us steal away

our dances made babies before Miley twerked

Muddy Waters sang"the blues had a baby they named it rock and roll"

Jazz was free …

Kamau Daood told us

"John Coltrane was a liberator-

liberated music from the shackles of form"

they try to say they discovered everything

but time is meaningless to a river as it washes to the sea

we birthed the blues

They only invented destruction

they are infants out of control

Baba Ngoma Osayemi Ifatunmise
Ngoma is a performance poet,multi instrumentalist,singer/songwriter,Artivist and paradigm shifter, who for over 50 years has used culture as a tool to raise socio-political and spiritual consciousness through work that encourages critical thought.

A former member of Amiri Baraka's "The Spirit House Movers and Players" and the contemporary freedom song duo"Serious Bizness",Ngoma weaves poetry and song that raises contradictions and searches for a solution to a just and peaceful world.

Ngoma was the Prop Slam Winner of the 1997 National Poetry Slam Competition in Middletown,CT and has been published in African Voices Magazine,Long Shot Anthology,The Underwood Review,Signifyin' Harlem Review,Bum Rush the Page/Def Poetry Jam Anthology,Poems on the Road to Peace-(Volumes 1,2,and 3) Yale Press and Let Loose On the World-Amiri Baraka at 75.

The Understanding Between Foxes and Light-Great Weather For Media and New Rain/Blind Beggar Press 35th Anniversary Issue. He was featured in the P.B.S spoken word documentary The Apropoets with Allen Ginsburg
Ngoma was selected as the Beat Poet Laureate of New York for 2021 by The National Beat Poetry Poetry Foundation

His newest work "I Didn't Come Here to Tap Dance (A Poetic Memoir) " is a collection of poems
spanning half a century inspired by a commitment to the Most High to create

Osunyoyin Alake Ifarike

We See You

To all you sons of Shango who
love women into their healing,
return the radiance to their eyes,
Place sister queens on pedestals,
high enough to see their path
open and clear in front of them...
Who resurrect and deliver the souls of
Oya's daughters from the obsidian
underworld of nightmares come true

We see you...

In homage to all you romantic Warriors
who chase souls, not skirts.
Who love the character of a sister
not just the presentation of her beauty.
Who see the magic of the Osun goddess in a
woman, not just the sway of her hips,
Who's fascinated by the inner workings of
her mind, and not just the soft roundness of her
body.

We see you.

For all you Kings who father children
not of your seed,
Who love, nourish, support, teach, raise,
discipline, strengthen, adore,
sons and daughters not of your making.
Who know that fatherhood is a gift.

We see you...
In honor of all of you Lions who walk
tall and proud in the front door of responsibility,
not the back door of cowardice.

To those who revere their ancestors in prayerful libations,
Who invoke the solution, not just the problem,
who speak in one voice,
find the high ground where we can all stand.
We see you.

In respect of you Visionary servants,
You Ogun men,
who bring evolution to the next generation
in spite of your own pain,
Who choose cooperation over competition,

peace over violence,
inclusion over alienation.

healing and growth
over bitterness, blame and anger,
We see you.

In celebration of all of you Luminaries
who do dishes, run a vacuum, dust, sweep
a floor, enlighten children during homework,
making sure its understood and gets done,

who massage feet, order take out or cook dinner.
Show that you understand that wife,
girlfriend, mother, daughter,
sister or aunt, is not just another word for maid,
slave, servant, or cook.

We see you.

In recognition of all of you Celestial Men,
You sons of Obatala who are
standing in the strength of divinity,
who are responsible fathers, good providers,
community leaders, quiet guardians, spiritual healers,
divine protectors, who are sweet, good and respectful
to all the elder men and women,
tender and patient with all the young
boys and girls in your life.

We see you.
To all of you MEN who are everything a man should be.
Who are always on your grown man,
Who feel invisible. You're not.
We see you and we love you.

The Blues

borrowed a blues riff and painted it into my sadness,

so it could rise 12 bars of hope

in 3,5,7 bent notes,

as a prayer to happiness...

Ain't nothing like the blues to make the bitter sound so sweet.

The Blues,

works in

soul creeping,

soul screeching,

mood altering guitar strings

echoing imperceptible nuances of my pain, where

Turquoise tortures escape in the water of my tears.

I stole the harmonic seventh,

chiseled it into my emotion,

singing,

so it could ascend in pentatonic freedom towards joy.
I coaxed call and response out of the hills,

to have someone to understand me,

Ring shout to keep me company,
and Indigo Ibo lamentations to help me

release it all, so my heart wouldn't be heavy and die.

The Blues left me in

Sapphire solitude,

Nurtured in Navy

and Cradled in Cobalt to heal.

Cause ain't nothing like the Blues to make a prayer so potent

or make the bitter sound so sweet

Spirit Jazz

A room in Heaven"s Mansion of Music
Showman's was full of spirits,
They didn't haunt it,
they jammed in it,
Their pictures over the bar,
rum, gin and other ethered
libations misted up to quench their souls.
Lionel
Sarah
Eckstine
Showman's, Harlem's 2nd cousin, twice removed from
the Apollo.
Their spirits shadowed hands, played bass,
tap mallots on steel pan,
Beat drums,
Called Africa stacatto out through the Congas.

No, these jazz spirits didn't haunt,
They inhabited
They lived,
They celebrated through
each riff, in each note.

These singing, creating musical masters, our ancestors in
craft,
Ella
Pearl
Betty,
had no unfinished business, it
was a continuation, an agreement, a pledge
in the eternal allegiance to genius shared in the magic of
music,
To the dance between notes,
Harmonies,
Major, minor and everything in between.
On Top
in the bottom beat.

Half and quarter note children of ancient African sounds reborn,
Twin
Triplet,
*Taiwo, Kehinde and Idowu,
Whisper secrets.
Pass on the magic in the music that sings in, down and through countless souls.
Reborn, re coupled in the real of now.
New marriages in this generation sing new songs with ancestral voices.

Stop by and hear prodigy reincarnated,
improvisation on less than a whim, born from an instant of inspiration.

Just one room in heaven's mansion of music
Showman's is sacred space!!!
In respect, don't forget to touch the ground and then your forehead when you
enter here, on 125th St
Pour a drop of liquor in libation,
a prayer of Thanksgiving for the gift hey left behind...that the faithful continue to give in return,
Remember, they are not ghost as long as their is music is played, they are Alive.

SOUL IS

Soul is collard greens, vornbread and pot liquor,

Soul is hearing James Brown's Say it loud I'm Black and and
I'm proud and tapping your toes dancing and nodding your
head, feeling proud,
 just as proud as you did
 the first time you heard it.
Soul is listening to instrumental music by John
Coltrane, Jimi Hendrix, Kool & the gang, and understanding
every word not sung but clear as
water, in every note of the music.

Soul is hearing your nana's voice saying "You can do it baby."
just when you need to hear it and she
passed away 5 years ago.

Soul is smiling at and greeting everyone
you see on the street on your walk to the subway.

Soul is watching the brothers drink beer on the
block and pouring out some on the ground saying "For those
of us who couldn't be here."

Soul is the priceless wisdom shared the barber
shop, the beauty salon and in Mama's kitchen
passed on to anyone who is in earshot of hearing.

Soul is Mama's tears of joy and surprise when the whole
family gathers to sing her Stevie Wonder's Happy Birthday
when she comes home after a long hard
 day at work.
Soul is the prayer and laying on of hands for a
loved one that was sick in the hospital and
seeing them rise up strong and LIVE GOOD
after their illness is cured.

Soul is looking at pictures of Malcolm X,
Martin Luther King, Kwame Touré, Ella Baker,

Fannie Lou Hammer and MarcusMarcus Garvey
and seeing the same warrior spirit, commitment, direction
and love for their people   burning through their eyes.

Soul is the African essence that shines in every
cell of our being and community no matter
what challenges we have overcome.

LOOK

YOU'RE NOT BLIND.

Look deeper and see past

the obsidian waters the slave ships

sailed across.

Look deeper than the beatings,

the bodies stacked like discarded rags,

Look deeper than the lies,

the rapes,

the insidious brain washings,

the black, blue and purple tortures.

Look deeper than how you were stripped of every trace of

Lyour identity,

your spirituality,

and your beauty.

Look back and see the astronomy you observed,wrote and

recorded,

Look back and see the medicine you gave the world,

Look back and see your science wrapped in the language of spirit,

Look back and read YOUR writings on the wall,

Look back and see the Mountains of the Moon,

See The first university ever founded inTimbuktu,

The Dogon cliff dwellings,

The Pyramids,

The Temples,

The echo of your Temples built all over the world,

Look back,

Close your eyes and remember

Then plant your feet in the earth,

Merge your head with heaven,

Hear your ancestors speak in every cell of your being,

Hear the Orisha speak in the whispering winds,

the scarlet cooking fires,

the silver rushing waters…

With purpose and intent Draw your power back into the sanctuary of your lungs, your muscles, your essence, your untapped strength,

Call the *Ase of *Obatala to purify your heart,

The Ase of *Orunmila to chart your destiny

The Ase of the divine connection in your own head to guide you to victory.
Break the chains of electric blue programing.

Break the gray chains of fear,

Break the charcoal chains of mindless misty paradigms that don't

serve you or our people.

Realize you haven't lost a thing.

It is yours, guarded by your genes,

Defended in your DNA,

Held in sacred safety by your always present ancestors.

Then step forward in the cloak of divine protection,

Divine endorsement,

Divine confirmation,

You can live in pain or your power,

Live in your power!!!

ASE!!

Osunyoyin Alake Ifarike , *is an African American anthro-photo-journalist, fine arts photographer, teaching artist, Osun priestess, Iyanifa, jewelry designer, sidereal astrologer, and poet. Osunyoyin has performed poetry in a variety of places from features at the Newyorican poets cafe to community festivals to the United Nations.*

George "LiteSkin" Escalante

<u>Being His Panic</u>

Alright,
Let's speak honestly…
Why do you hate me?
I know it's not the music or the culture that I'm a part;
Definitely know it's not the anger
That you put in my heart:
It couldn't be the bagginess of my jeans;
That's none of your concern:
Why would it be the fact that a voice is heard,
But now it's my turn;
Wonder if it's my speech
Or what you call an impediment:
Could it be that I'm knowledge
Filled with energy?
Is it my walk
Or what you call a sway?
Or that I broke through your stereotypes
To do things my way?
Is it that I spend time on my corner,
Got you watching my every move?
Or that I'm talented
And I ain't got a damn thing to prove?
Nah,
I know exactly what it is…
Is that I lead instead of follow:
I mentally control my tomorrows;
Speak with authority…
I can't be held:
I live what you tell,
And it's called hell;
My passion is stronger than your desire:
My goals have always been put
In a level that's higher;
But I accomplish them
And run over the hurdles in my path:
You hate me

Because I do it with strength and a laugh;
Looks easy,
That's why your depression is so manic:
Plus my race...
Has always been His Panic;
And this Lati-Knows
Everything you plot:
You hate me because you want what I got;
But you blame it on my tongue,
Because you say it's loose:
But most of all you despise me
Because I can reproduce!

LITESKIN 1:23

How Many Times...

Desensitized eyes are always flooded with lies,
So when I size up situations
I first look for truths that are disguised;
Are we still looking up at skies?
Are bended knees how we rise?
We've said prayers for years,
And are still in back of life's lines!
"The meek shall inherit the earth"
But since birth,
We've been plagued with pain
So I ask,
"What's that worth?"
How has hurt changed our positions?
It's strengthened our skins
But hasn't stopped hell from sizzling;
Our life lines are flickering,
Batteries are dying:
Yet the wicked are still bickering,
Complaining while firing;
Our people AND guns:
Affecting family funds,
While taking our sons;
Broad daylight lynchings:
Back home for dinner,
Without missing a drum:
Sum it all up…
The equations are still the same;
Adding stress while subtracting more lives:
Blood thirsty systems' dividends
Are only different by name;
They have weakness in their veins,
Hatred masks their insecurities:
On top they remain,
And still continue their buffoonery:
There's power in words we speak;
I'm far from minor…
I don't respond to, "minority"!
I don't see supreme

And don't honor your, "supremacy"!
Since we have the tendency
To only react to fatalities,
I have a question...
How many times must we hear,
"I CAN NOT BREATHE"!

LITESKIN 1:23

I Spit

I spit for Kalief Browder
Trayvon and Sandra;
There are so many questions With no clear answers:
I spit for Garner, Gray
And so many others;
Whose remains are mourning children
With destroyed mothers:
I spit for my brother;
Who spiritually died behind a cell
Released from that system
And departed his shell:
I spit for Sean Bell;
"Til Death Do Them Part"
Didn't get to the alter
To give her his heart:
I spit to spark…
Fires for our young
That all feel abandoned;
Miseducation and handcuffs
Have become standard:
I spit against the cancer
Spread through our homes;
Flood the hood with drugs
And nickle plated chrome:
For that,
We must spit to our own;
Feed our people with the truth
Be more responsible
When you're in that booth:
Our roots are of warriors
Trained and ready for war;
So I ask you,
What are you spitting for?

  LITESKIN 1:23

"Letter To Gil"

Dear Mr.
Gil Scott-Heron,
You became an audible hero
When most were just stuck on heroin:
Better men rose to the challenge;
When you parted for that poetical palace,
Kings took sips from their chalice:
Soldiers saluted your existence;
You spoke to the educators
And the misfits:
So intricate with your idiosyncrasies;
Deliberate so
Idiots can be in sync and see:
You planted a seed with that…
"Message to Messengers";
So I took heed…
And I let it register:
So ahead of your time…
Rappers today
Still recycle your lines;
You defined the fact
That greed got us declined:
Rejected by society
So we allow private agencies
To color us blind;
Lack of spines…
Got us falling for anything:
Makes sense
Of why we praise our enemies;
Your energy…
Could've sparked a movement:
Where we fight for ours;
Put a stop to the abusement:
Instead,
We allow crumbs for soothing
And let them move in
At their leisure for their amusement;

We've become stupid!
Since you passed,
Knowledge has been negated:
Because our current orators
Seem conceptually constipated;
We've been fumigated and pepper sprayed
So our vision is impaired,
Proven by what we say:
Nowadays,
Everybody is "Little";
Not just by title:
That's expected with
Our cross-dressed Ameriscared idols;
Confusion is vital,
Our people: Suicidal:
Supposed leaders now twerk on frontlines
For some views;
What are we to do to revitalize pride?
Feeble sheep have become accidental spies:
Maybe the revolution will be televised;
Because they introduced Facebook Live!

LITESKIN 1:23

MESSAGE IN A BOTTLE

Chemi-Kills in the air
Have spared absolutely no one;
Human actions are the ammo,
So we ourselves are the gun:
Listen to that,
"Pop U Late Son"
As a Con
Trolls the nation;
Govern mental decisions
That causes bloody Red Rum!
Reflective image,
The mirror is blurry:
So is our future...
Our oxygen is dirty;
Our trees are falling,
Water is tainted:
Quakes caused by man
So Earth gets a face-lift!
The basics...
We've destroyed Mother Nature!
Her radiance affected by radiation;
She's returning the favor!
Who's left to save her...
With our technical advances?
Were told about dying-saurs:
Our asteroids are now cancers!
Not speaking astrology
But apologies are well in order;
Because this new world
Should be on trial for human slaughter!

LITESKIN 1:23

"Read Between The Lines"

Why is
Everybody so
Anxious to
Run from
Everything?
Based on
Every minorities'
Culture…we should be
Open to
Manual laboring:
Intelligence is not for
Niggas
Gukes or
Spics but
Only for
Bosses who
Live
In
Nice rich
Districts!

LITESKIN 1:23

Sincere Letter (Dear Women)

Dear Women;

On my behalf, I would like to apologize: I would like to apologize for all the snickering teeth; Name calling beneath idiotic believes that women are just meat: Ignorant phrases of, *"Mami, can you hit me off?"* And other half-thought remarks that you come across; Half-witted questions of, *"Shorty, can I get your math?"* Or, *"Damn sweetheart, you got a banging ass"* **No Class!** Noises you would hear from animals in cages: Now, I ask for forgiveness for us not acting our ages: ***"Hell hath no fury like a woman scorned"*** And it seems we've forgotten from where we were born; I apologize to my Mother, sister, wife, and daugthers: And all women that give birth to us; I'm sorry for the harassment you go through on a daily basis: And for all that you've done, I am very gracious; I hope you accept my apology, And in all honesty, I want you to know I'm so glad that you're a part of me; And I am a part of you: Together we make a bond; And without you women, Us men couldn't go on!

Love Always,
Real Men

LITESKIN 1:23

George "LiteSkin" Escalante's

Born and raised in New York City's Lower East Side, LiteSkin (Living It Through Every Situation Known In Nature) is a HipHop/SpokenWord artist who exudes passion and grit in everything he spits. Since young, he's been focused on empowering all who listen with his ability to bend words and use multi-leveled meanings with his wordplay. Appropriately titled the, "WordSmith With A Purpose", he has spread his messages for many years. A lifetime advocate for youth, he has dedicated all his professional and artistic work in advancing the betterment of the young and all those around him. Lite has performed in and hosted countless events throughout NYC and New York State and has left his mark on all microphones he's touched. His art and talents can be found on all musical streaming sites and YouTube.

Instagram:
https://www.instagram.com/realliteskin123/

FaceBook:
https://www.facebook.com/LITESKIN123

YouTube:
https://www.youtube.com/user/lesliteskin

Twitter: https://twitter.com/LITESKIN321

Queen Jua

This Crown

You see this crown
It never comes down
It may tilt a little bit
But baby I'm built to wear it.

I didn't come here to convince you who I am
You see me
You feel me
There is power my tone
Yes I'm strong when I stand
Respect I command
You'd be best to leave the other side of me alone

My crown was once specks of dust
I collected as growing pains
I maintained my crown kept it from rust
And formed it with all the love and truth I've gained

Shines so bright fits so tight you can't see the rubies and emeralds, gold and diamonds
Custom made, custom fit and compliments any dress or pants I'm styled in
You can't touch this

The perfectly imperfect crown
The no regrets and worth it to me crown
The weight of this crown can only be carried by me
The weft the depth too much for just any body
Hell yeah it's heavy

I am she, she is me I wear my crown proudly
Giver of life, mother of more, still building my great legacy
Call me Queen call me Ohema, Tiwa or just her majesty
I know who I am, and the truth becomes me

I stand on the shoulders of great women just like me
I inherited this, this crown was passed down to me.
First manifested as thought and now a reality.
I am royal, across all lands, I am the holy trinity, knowledge wisdom and understanding
only 5% of you can see me.

This crown is my headgear when I'm at war
Battle scars to prove it, Yet I've conquered even more
They've tried to defeat me thought I'd lose it
But the God in me can't be brought down convicted or ignored, this is soul armor you can't bruise it

Yeah, You see this crown
It never comes down
It may tilt a little bit
But baby I'm born to wear it

Brother Be Still

Brother be still when the day awakens
and your mind is unsure
When uncertainty riddles your head
and you need strength to endure

Brother be still when you move,
calm in your spirit steady in your motion
Every step intentional and deliberate
to dodge this world's negative notions

Brother be still before you decide,
before you pop off, before you react
In a place designed to destroy you,
you've got to keep your thoughts in tact

Brother be still
cause sometimes you've got ants in your pants
Find yourself while chasing your doubts
stop making I can, can'ts

Don't you know who you are?
Don't you know we sisters see you?
My Brother we need you
We've got you
We love you

Brother be still to relax your jaw and open your fists, stay ready and aware, but know that the power in your presence forever exists

Brother be still with your words and careful with your speech. Know how influential you are, with the hearts your tone may reach.

Then also be still in your touch.
When you hold us, when you love us, it means so much.
My brother be still, as we all admire your browns and tans kissed by the sun, sexy and tough,
Makes us remember it's you we must respect,
in YOU we must trust

Brother be still within YOU,
cause this planet could not BE without YOU.
Our Fathers, sons, husbands, brothers, protectors of your sisters, sources of truth

Gods

Brother please be still
That you may still BE

For The Family

I can feel you reminding me to be strong
Reminding me the pain won't be long
Telling me it's up to me to keep it together
as I've always done,
For the family

Can you imagine what it feels like
to hold sand in your hands?
Trying to hold on to as much as you can
But it keeps slipping through your fingers?

I'm not built for this
I can't do this
I'm gonna break
Let me try to keep it together

I want to go to the highest mountain and wail.

Wail, until I have no more tears
Wail for the coming years
Without you.

But, I can still feel YOU encouraging me to stay strong
Reminding me the pain won't be long
Insisting that I keep it together
For the family.

But it's more like holding 1000 pounds above my head.
Are you grasping what I said?
I AM HOLDING 1000 POUNDS ABOVE MY HEAD.

I'm not built for this
I can't do this
I'm gonna break
GOTTA keep it together

I feel like I'm going insane
So much confusion in my brain
But the family is watching
They're hurting too,
So I'm gonna do what I gotta do,
Gotta stay the strong one
In honor of you
For the family.

You owe me big time for this
This was never on our conversation list
(My aunt, my friend I could confide in you)
You always gave loving advice on what to do,
But, You never prepared me to be without
YOU

I'm not built for this
I can't do this
I'm gonna break

But I WILL keep it together

Cause you'd have it NO other way.

The Crush

I wanna know you in a way that I know my self,
Speak intelligent and woke King
Impress me with your mental wealth

I wanna listen to your voice to feel and hear your soul
Let me learn from you, I wanna build with you, truth be told

I wanna be a vision of your favorite melody,
I want you to feel warm colors when you think of me.
Allow me to give you comfort like never before
I wanna be more than you could ever wish for

I wanna be that sweet taste on the inside of both our lips
How crazy is this energy Especially between our hips?

Your swagg, your vibe, the God in you
Got a sister throbbing about what you really can do.

Cum explore my hills and valleys I'll show you where to go
Frequently there's tugging daddy just try to take it slow,

You feel it, It's orgasmic, I...

Just wanna make you smile even when you don't want to,

For you I'll BE LOVE, that's all I wanna do.

My Love

You are every love song I've seen myself in
Songs of forever togethers and meant to bes, Soulmates and flaming twins

I dream of you

You are the melody of a jazz song, the boom and the bip. I move with every tone every sound, as I girate my waist and hips

You're the dutty whine and grind of soca and reggae, sweet like sorrel you shine bright like Brooklyn's colors on Labor Day

You are the drums calling from the motherland in the form of Afrobeats, familiar like home welcoming you with undeniable reach

You're the spicy and hot of salsa and meringue sexy and flirtatious, you move with intent yet you're always gracious

You're the grit and truth of Hip Hop and rap. Every bar, every word with a hot ass beat making dope ass tracks

My lonely keeps me focused as I tell myself these things. That I'm the one I've been listening and looking for all this time it seems.

This...
This is LOVE

I am the rhythm and sound of all music
The ability to travel across the globe, I am universal all while the message is understood and the stories are being told

I AM LOVE
GOD IS LOVE

My bare body the curvy Bass and beating drums, hands clapping, fingers popping, the larynx is in use somehow
Songs in my head in my heart this is me in my element in my oneness in my divineness in my now

I am in Love
I am listening
I am dancing
I am free

LOVE IS FREEDOM
LOVE IS GOD
And GOD
Well GOD IS ME

Ultraviolet (haiku)

Sun, and all the pink
Faces hide under it to
burn away; themselves

Music

Why does music love me so much?
Huh?
Why does music know me so well?
Huh?
Why does music hug me through my ears when I'm happy or when I feel fear?
Calming me

I don't mean to be crude but music sounds better in the nude. When I'm alone like I wanna be or how it gotta be, music is there
In the tv on the phone through my ceiling fan and when it's quiet
Always finding a way to get to me, go through me, play, or say what I need to hear, or the tone I need to feel.

I hear music in the bird's morning song in my children's voices and in my grandmother's hello, in kind words and in moments of love, and pain. I hear music when the wind blows and I know inside I'm protected.

I don't know about you but these devices are listening
Cause when I'm missing…well…music comes through
Most days when I awake there's a song in my head, when I recognize it, I've gotta play it or sing it or, I just might miss what music is trying to say

Music affects my hands and my hips most times I don't even notice, then my voice wants to match what I'm hearing, if I let it I'll lose focus, while I sing and dance in my head. Wait, What was I doing?

As a young girl music knew I was attracted to love, so music carried me through my journeys of sadness and joy with a nudge to remember who I am, while blocking away the negative noise.

Music is life and love, lets me know God loves me all while playing the soundtrack of my soul, there are no coincidences, or mysterious controls, things are as they should be. Just listen.

Music is in sincere apologies, and in rage, music is a hug from someone that loves you, and in memories, music is in a kiss, music is in the rain, in the sunshine and in the special moments that happen again and again.

Why does music love me so much?
Huh?
Why does music know me so well?
Huh?
Why does music hug me through my ears when I'm happy or full of fear?
Calming me

Flying Home

I'm in the air flying feeling closer to my Grandma
as I begin to cry,
I'm above the clouds feeling like heaven is nearby.

It's sounds crazy but if it would be God's will
to take this vessel down,
I would accept my fate and choose to be with her now,
If it's not God's plan then today would not be my date.
It's just the days to come living without my Grandma that I truly hate.

All my life I've longed to be like she was, a true pillar of strength, honesty and love

She was never a burden to me and never a chore
It was me who needed her in my life and I realize it even more

I wanna be alone, crowded rooms seem
to only mask my increasing pain
As I smile, laugh and grin I know my life will never be the same

I'm in the air flying feeling closer to my Grandma
as I begin to cry,
I'm above the clouds feeling like heaven is nearby.

I miss you Grandma like I'd miss air,
and I feel like I can't breathe
I realize God that I'm being selfish
but I just want her here with me.

Forgive me cause I know this is all in the Universe's design.
Please guide me through a righteous walk so I can see her if just
one
more
time.
 I want to stretch my arms up to the sky
just to touch her face.
Just one more time Grandma, before this plane touches down
and leaves this space

I'm in the air flying feeling closer to God,
Please take care of my Angel
Because letting her go is unbearable and REALLY hard.

I LOVE YOU GRANDMA

Queen Jua

Queen Jua is the owner and operator of Queen Jua's World, a multifaceted venture that includes her role as manager, producer, consultant and curator for the legendary Hip Hop pioneers, The Last Poets. Since 2015, she has managed co-founder Abiodun Oyewole's solo career, contributing to the group's ongoing legacy in the genre. Under her management, The Last Poets have enjoyed numerous performance and speaking engagements both in the U.S. and internationally.

In addition to her work with The Last Poets, Queen Jua is the producer and co-host of "Poets Haven Sundays," a biweekly event featuring notable poets such as Jessica Care Moore and J. Ivy. She has also hosted "Danny Simmons Presents Def Poetry Reunion," celebrating the legacy of the iconic "Def Poetry Jam" in locations like Jamaica Queens and Martha's Vineyard.

An accomplished poet herself, Queen Jua has performed at various venues, including the Wadsworth Atheneum's Amistad Cultural Centre and The Firehouse Harlem. As an ordained minister, she offers ministerial services, weddings, and poetry recitals, showcasing her diverse talents and commitment to the arts.

The photo
Credit
Frank Crum
(City of Tampa)

Charles Daniel Perry Jr, CP Maze

My brainstorms are savage toothless ruthless vagrants with
very bad tempers. A never-land
of never mind: You could never silence the saliva on an I
won't choke back words or bite my Tongues-telling the hands
of God, that Christians are repping their denominations
so hard, that they're now throwing up gang signs in Gods
names. Flocks of congregations are loading up their pistols
with proverbs pointing fingers like BLA BLA BLAW: If the
books in the bible were neighborhood street blocks, know
that when the Saints came marching in, they came in,
slanging communion like crack rock. All of the holy rollers
are street hustlers.

Judas is a jump boi jacking chalices
from any last supper table for any 30
pieces of silver he could find.

Apocalypse is fresh off of parole looking to kill any
& all *Revelations* that are caught hanging outside
of its bible books hood after dark. *Adam & Eve* are a bunch
of habitual criminals bouncing bad checks that the Garden
of Eden can't quite cover. Good & Evils, *Tree of Knowledge,*
is a sophomore in college, double majoring in *Human
Resources* & *Political Science,*
minoring in *Silence,*
some souls just need saving. & I'll be damned if
Daniel ain't shooting up heroine in the Lion's Den again.

a mover & shaker *Moses* is moving weed-bowl bundles
upon bundles of burning bushes by the pound,
moving mountains upon mountains of Mount Sinai crack
parting red seas slanging kilos of cocaine baking soda cut.

whoever said *Mary Magdalene* was just some harlot hooker
whore or prostitute
probably never ever not never noticed at the *Last Supper*
she was the fiery redhead

sitting at the right hand of the Son of God.
ohhh *Mary, Mother of Jesus, Mother Mary,*
Mary the Blessed Virgin
is a high school hallway substitute teacher teaching safe
Sex-Education
issuing immaculate conceptions contraceptives

fidgety restless antsy *Hallelujahs*
have been all night waiting to get into
a club called *Noah's Arc.*

there's no entry fee nor no cover charge
feel free to coat-check your Halos at the door
with the cute coat check girl named *Karma.*

John the Baptist is so dump-a-body-down-by-the-river
gangsta
that the streets nicknamed him *"Holy Water."*

the *Twelve Disciples* are an in & out of jail-
-street-smart-bunch of gang bangers with bachelor's degrees
...scholars from the School of Hard Knocks
...scholars who are classically trained in the Liberal Arts
of the Dope-Fiend & fluently speaks junky

these *Twelve Disciple* street scholars
have enough soldiers discipline to break bread with *Peace*
or go all in off into an all-out Gangsters War
where no one's safe
even your kids can come up missing

Adam & Eve are enjoying Apple Martini's
at a happy hour in the hood
Psalms is parking lot pimping hoes right out of their
hallelujahs
Samson and Delilah are fighting over elbow room in a taxi

Book of Genesis just sent a Valentine's to the *Big Bang*
Theory

Signed Sincerely Yours,
Veni Vidi Vici

p.s
look Lawd take a week off you look like you can use some rest

Charles Daniel Perry Jr, artistically known as CP Maze, has a story worthy of the history books. A decorated Marine Corps veteran with a heart full of muse, a mind storm of Marine Corps memories, and an artistic repertoire as well trained and mature as the marine smoldering inside. Rankings of 3rd & 4th in the World for Performance Poetry; his honesty, identity, and creativity have been encoded with that of an outlaw. Currently a student in The University of Houston's Creative Writing Poetry program, Maze is determined to leave our world better than we were given it.
Contact Info:
cpmaze@gmail.com
www.faceboook/cpmaze
www.instagram.com/cpmaze

Rewop Be

Dam Bass

Im jealous of her
the way he makes her sang
the way he touches her
how he looks at her
The way she says his name
And it makes me feel some type of way

It should be me he's plucking
it should be me he's fucking
I told y'all I'm jealous of her
him n her go all night
with her everything is right
soft n hard
slow n fast
she gets fingers n tongue
n smacks on the ass
while I wait patiently for the moment to pass
And it makes me feel some type of way
I wanna be in her place
can u put me on your face
See I watch as he slides on her pulls off n hammers on
I just wanna bend some way find a place in his song
n I know I'm wrong
but it makes me feel some type of way

I watch as he touches her tuners and rubs up n down her neck
n with every lick n reverb
I'm drawn closer to his sex n
I wanna say can I be next

See his alternate picking n strumming of her
causes lickings n cumming from me
so I'm jealous of her

I want him to myself
but without her
he wouldn't be his best self
n it makes me feel some type of way
Dam I told u I'm jealous of her
she always with him
that should be me in his hands
across his chest
laying on his abs,
can that be me he grabs
slapping on this ass
strumming on my strings
making me sing
dam bass
if he put it in my face I would kiss it
and it makes me feel some type of way

I'm jealous of what cums from her
the look of satisfaction in his eyes
I'm hypnotized
watching him with her
N it makes me feel some type of way

We Still Here

Enthralled with black soul n black seed unaware of black
need   but blacks bleed
like weed   n california.
Everywhere
black hair black hair change
rearrange , foreign, strange,
stran-ge
smother black sunray to the gods
black fake black facad
Black snob bourgeois odd
give nods
like sod cut from their root
black shades black suits
only recruits.   not real
not black feel   black fuel
gas for others,
black mothers   black mothers die
no
black mothers cry
no
black mothers watch their children fly
with no direction   with no connection
to black love black hugs
black like black right
only black songs give us life
give us fight,   give us fright,
music with no sight   no flight   only hell
blacks sell. blacks sale
cakes n socks   Weed n rocks
Pills n glocks,   cars n cock   hoes on blocks
blacks sail   streets n allies,   mountains n valley,
blacks rallie, rise   blacks protest n emprovise
black pride.
black pride
be strong. be long. be gone
erased   replaced   with black face

no black soul
black waste
chasing fools gold
n black body.   now parts
black love now art   to be viewed
not had   black dads
black dads far n few,
school, sports, streets, music, or prison issue
black dad,   foriegn to most of u
black new   new black
act
all the time   at anytime
change they morals, they mind
they beliefs they grind
depending on the time
the space   the place
the race   the case
Black face.   blacks face
crime   hard times   walking the line
Stupid rhymes. Paying fines. Throwing up signs
Getting in a bind. Running out of time
N losing their mind.   But we still here...

Scorpio-licious

She dwells in femininity with every sway of her hips
she slips on sexy with every outfit
she's Lena Horne and eartha kitt
Call her Dorothy dandridge in Josephine baker clothes she knows her power
she's a flower with lavender scent
she passion and all its colors
she's a lover, a hugger,
she demands your attention your respct she's sex
sensuous sultry
she dwells in femininity
feelings   she's revealing
healing hopeful inspiring desiring
she stands head high
fly floetry
poetry in every step
she rep black brown chocolate light dark
she like bark. root
she cute calm psalms
she proverbs good herbs,
she you she me she us
she dont make a fuss. she cuss
quietly   silently
she peace
she dwell in femininity
she ritual spiritual
n voodoo she woo you soothe you cool you
when you upset
she make you sweat
swoon she be the moon
maple syrup sweet
she like fresh air in the heat,
she stop your heartbeat,
she bittersweet
she out your reach
she dwell in femininity

she complex n simple
she's a smile with dimples
she enticing,
like icing she gives life flavor
she gods favor .... She Scorpio-licious...

Jada

Jada changed the game of cheating with one word
kicked all other explanations for fucking someone else
to the curb
took the wrong out of a wrongdoing
to justify her screwing
another man
a younger man
someone other than
her husband n mate
decided she was gone control n create
the narrative for her actions
she went to somebodies book for that one
n that gives me satisfaction
being a poet n all
That shit took some gall
some planning as well
Maybe even a spell
Cause why else would will smith slap Chris on oscar night
instead of beating august Alsinas ass on sight for running his
mouth
for being hurt n choosing to talk about
what was between them,
her him n him
that is if Will was even completely aware,
n I'm all for showing a young person u wanna help or care
But beware
cause August was Jaden's friend
n Jada's how why n when
just don't make sense
U don't sleep with the children that interact with your child
That action in itself was completely foul
even if Will was n agreement with the play
u just don't condone, lay nor display those types of moves onto
or into your family
Unless you don't care
or maybe I'm just not aware
of the demons y'all praying too

N I'm completely ok with no longer following u
Cause I question your actions
n I find dissatisfaction
in what y'all doing to each other n your kids
I hope it was worth it whatever sacrifice y'all did
Cause it fucked most of your fans up
N I acknowledge I don't know what's in your cup
or your shoes
but I can say for most jada your entanglement
had us all dazed n confused
Cause it wasn't appropriate or ok
Will, August,
or Jayden will never trust u or a woman the same way
Or maybe u not aware that to men young n old u like
Lisa ray
Diamond forever, that goes for every role
 u ever played
 Carla peaches Rome, Annie n sonji
 Sloan Lisa Fish Lena n Niobe
 Some not on my list but u get what I'm saying
 When u said it was an entanglement I thought u was playing

Rewop Be

The name is Rewop, check it out in reverse
Rewop's goal is to create, share, hone, write, learn, and educate while being innovative, original, spiritual, political, radical and revolutionary, bringing her craft of spoken word to the masses.

Rewop is originally from Oakland California and currently resides in Atlanta Georgia but Cincinnati is where her poetry performances began.

Rewop"s road has become entitled "The Coochie Chronicles" and as a spoken word artist, writer of the book, core cast member and primary writer of the play she's bringing Coochie to you. So get you some cause It's a beautiful thing.
Rewop is a member of Adams Rib led by the queen of spoken word Georgia Me and she is also apart of the Historic Punany Poets led by the amazing Jessica Holter and she produced and co-wrote Coochie Chronicles the spoken word play with Jennie "BlackButterfly" Wright.
Rewop can be found on tours nationally alongside Georgia Me, Jessica Holter, Abyss, Redstorm Chicago, and a host of other amazing poets, she currently resides in College Park, Georgia and is currently sharing the Coochie with the world nationally if you would like some,

Rewop is available for all events and can be contacted at 678-651-0456 or via email at sefluv@yahoo.com

CeLillianne Green

Home

Without notice or warning
Quietly, like the new day dawning

He opens the door of my heart
Then moves inside to the deepest part

This is no ordinary day
I am clear God sent him my way

He arrives at the perfect time
My heart is wide open and perfectly primed

He makes himself at home right away
His heart beat tells me of his desire to stay

There is not much I need to say
The beat of my heart sounds the same way

We share a soul vibration, a perfect tone
On a frequency heard by us— and us alone

He hears it and I hear it too
The sound of pure love, absolute and true

In this pure love, we are home
From this love, we never roam

I Woke Up

Last night, I fell into a deep sleep
I didn't dream. I didn't hear a peep

Today, I woke up in my home
I am alive. I am not alone.

I woke up as a woman, Black and free
That's who I am. That's me

A Black woman with 1 brain to think
2 eyes to blink
For the right man, I will smile and wink

Today, I woke up with ancestral memories
Centuries of history

Memories which can bring a smile or a frown
Deep memories in which to drown

Today, I woke up with 2 knees to kneel and pray
2 ears to listen to what others say

I woke up to the weekly sounds of trash removal
Expected sounds. No need for approval

Today, I woke up with 2 arms to hold on tight
2 legs to walk away from an unprovoked fight

I woke up with 1 mouth to open or close
And 1 perfectly centered nose

A nose able to inhale and exhale
Without breath, life fails

George Floyd exhaled his last breath, last year
In 2020, the world watched, and there were tears

Today, I woke up to a policeman tried for Floyd's death
A policeman convicted for causing Mr. Floyd's last breath

Piercing Eyes

I am a little Black girl with piercing eyes
Afraid to release tears I must cry

I hold my hands across my heart
Keeping my soul from being torn apart

I am a little Black girl with power inside
But, I have only been taught to survive

I need to be taught how to rise and thrive
Then, I will move through this world truly alive

I am a little Black girl making my way
Listening intently for what God has to say

Sometimes I confuse what God says
I wonder if God is alive or dead

Yet, in the spirit of who I am
I know God has a master plan

Sadly, I have no one to guide me or to help me grow
Yet, there's so much I want to know

That's why I focus my piercing eyes on you
Hoping you will teach me what I should do

My piercing eyes you are unable to meet
I am someone you will not greet

You have seen me and felt my piercing eyes
You have looked at me as someone to despise

I know why you look at me as you do
I can look through to the depth of you

I see you too are afraid to cry
I know exactly why
Why you don't live, but you are afraid to die

For me, death is nothing to fear
I have often asked death to come near

I know death is a transition to another space and time
There, my ancestors thrive and are just fine

Yes, death comes as the ultimate release
Release to the place of ancestral peace

In that peace, there is an ancestral prize
— Piercing eyes, no longer despised

Water

Don't come to me weak like creek water
Come to me knowing I'm God's daughter

Come to me like a river flowing into the sea
Come to me with your heart open and absolutely free

Don't come to me like a meandering stream
Come to me with the power of all of your dreams

Come to me with the serenity of a placid lake
Come to me knowing our love is at stake

Don't come to me like a puddle I can step over
Come to me with the mystery of a 4-leaf clover

Come to me ready to stand by my side
Come to me balanced with humility and pride

Don't come to me like white water rapids out of control
Come to me connected to the depth of your soul

Come to me like an ocean deep and wide
Come to me in the fullness of your stride

Don't come to me tentative or unsure
Come to me knowing our love is the cure

Come to me with the power of Niagara Falls
Come to me dignified, standing tall

Don't come to me like a ripple from a pebble tossed in a lake
Come to me with the energy of a wave just before it breaks

Come to me like a river overflowing its banks
Come to me giving God praise and thanks

Don't come to me like intermittent rain
Come to me willing to release your tears and pain

Come to me as a refreshing summer downpour
Come to me with the certainty that I'll want more

Don't come to me laden with self-doubt
Come to me knowing what you're about

Come to me like the rising tide of the River Nile
Come to me with sunshine in your smile

Don't come to me like a slow moving glacier
in the arctic freeze
Come to me bringing the warmth of a tropical breeze

Come to me in the fullness of time
Come to me with clarity and with a sound mind

Don't come to me unbending like the Strait of Gibraltar
Come to me to build our sacred altar

Come to me like a port where I can anchor myself
Come to me with the knowledge of your spiritual wealth

Don't come to me like steam dissipating from a hot spring
Come to me fully prepared to make my heart sing

Come to me long like the Mississippi River
Come to me with a love that will make me shiver

Don't come to me like a body of water man diverted to create
Come to me with the power of a love that cannot wait

Come to me like the water God created to sustain life
Then and only then will I be your wife

CeLillianne Green is an internationally known poet, as well as a lawyer, teacher, and speaker. A graduate of Drexel and Howard Universities, she was Editor-in-Chief of the Howard Law Journal, and is admitted to the Bar in PA, NY, DC, and MD. Her legal career includes a federal clerkship, Wall Street law firm associate, an AUSA who tried cases from misdemeanors to 1st degree murders, and argued appeals. Ms. Green was a co-founder of a private law practice, served as a legislative counsel, a mediator, and as an instructor in law schools and public schools.

In 2001, Ms. Green wrote her first poem, *Because I Love You,* which she published in 2003 with no thought of writing more poetry. In 2005, more poems started. In 2009, the Kirwan Institute for the Study of Race and Ethnicity recognized her as a Social Justice Thought Leader for her poem, *Lifted*. Her first book, *That Word,* an epic poem was published in 2010 and it was selected in 2015 by the DC Black Theatre Festival for a Staged Reading. Ms. Green adapted *That Word* as playwright and producer. Her recording, *CeLillianne Says* and her poetry collection, *A Bridge, The Poetic Primer on African and African American Experiences* published in 2011 and 2015, respectively. Her e-book, *Marching Orders & She Rose* was published in 2013.

For the 150th Anniversary of the District of Columbia Emancipation Day, she penned *The Call of Freedom,* and recited it at the Martin Luther King, Jr. Memorial in 2012. Ms. Green wrote the 50th Anniversary poem, *Civil and Right*, which is published in "Moving America Toward Justice, The Lawyers Committee for Civil Rights Under Law 1963-2013." She read *Civil and Right* at the Premiere Kick-Off & Awards Reception in the U.S. Institute of Peace. In January 2016, Ms. Green recited her original work, *The Cycle of Life* for the Julian Bond Celebration of Life Convocation at Lincoln University. July 9, 2016, she presented the Commemorative Poem, *They Prayed* at the Bicentennial of the African

Methodist Episcopal Church in Phila., PA. In 2016, she was also inspired to write *The Present* to mark the occasion of the opening of the Smithsonian National Museum of African American History and Culture. Ms. Green wrote *A Special Place 150 Years Bold* for the Anniversary of her alma mater, Howard University School of Law in 2019. *The Victorious K.B.J., Ketanji Brown Jackson*, her tribute to the first Black woman appointed to the Supreme Court of the U.S. was published in 2022. She debuted this poetic essay in the "First Monday In October 2022" at the Thurgood Marshall Center Trust, Inc.

Ms. Green has been interviewed on radio and TV, quoted in newspapers, and cited in law journal articles. She has contributed to anthologies, documentaries, online publications, and has been invited to speak to public schools, universities, and organizations. Ms. Green has appeared in Jazz Festivals, and in 2023, she produced *CeLillianne Green's Evening of Poetry & Jazz* which is available on her YouTube channel. In sum, Ms. Green's poetry and prose are about life, love, spirituality, relationships, history, and politics. Contact her at www.CeLillianneGreen.com.

Toni Hamilton

God, it's me

One little small breath of your Essence,
one dancing, reaching, rolling wave of your ocean,

Let's talk, God.
Hear me!
Let's talk about the world…
the energetic cacophony
of hearts and demons vying for empowerment.

Let's talk about fragileness
and things so big they draw awe,
powerlessness so defeating that it births
a deafening silence of paralysis
cause we just can't figure out how to correct it, change it,
transform it into something worth building upon.
God, I want insight into the juxtaposition of beauty and heartache.
What were you thinking, God?!

Does it matter if we destroy it
ALL?!

It's

It's been my refuge, my joy,
my medicine,
my conversation piece,
recording of history
an echo of my ancestor's thoughts,
feelings,
woes,
hopes and dreams,
my teacher,
my time machine,
a spiritual bath cleansing the abuse, mistakes
and painful answers to questions I never asked.
It's been my spaceship transporting me to lands of beauty,
Magical sun streams, rain beams and breathtaking waterfalls
riding the waves of possibility,
Steering my heart to its rightful home.
A medicine bag with ancient, divine healing essence,
the knife that cuts out lies,
thread that repairs my tattered soul,
salve that soothes the bruises,
my witness, my voice, my clarion call,
our talking drum,
motivator,
map of the unknown realms within me,
my silver chord to God,
the straw I sip my ethos through…
It's Music.

THAT

That stops me within the moment
Changes my energy
Brings me wonder and awe
Softens me
Ignites something – Love
That washes through me

That!
Makes me feel grateful that I am alive
Despite the mysteries
That makes me feel like it's worth pushing forward
Cause it teaches me, reminds me,
there is something greater than myself
Greater than pain, confusion, heartache
Moments of powerlessness

Something so magnificent and wonderful,
So full of love and rightness and good
That it gifts us with glowing moons
Encircled with red, yellow, blue rainbow rings
Flowing crystal flashes falling from the night sky
blanketing the earth
Prism drops of water called rain that dance pitter patter
Oh, so soft drumming songs that replenish the earth and soothe my soul

Golden light streams that cascading through the trees, through my window creating patterns like Adinkra symbols and signs dancing through the ocean's waves illuminating the depths of creation warming this existence with a glow radiant love like that
That!
That!
Beauty.

The Frozen Part

The frozen part of me is probably the best part.
The part that's been stuck,
encased in inertia,
the part that will soar, fly,
tumble, dive and float within creative freedom.
The part that speaks unabashedly without concern of disdain or retribution
Believing that I am free to be me.
To make mistakes,
To not have to get it right, less I might be attacked, or harmed by those that disagree.

The frozen part of me is genius, raw, loving, honest, powerful and filled with love, bubbling with joy and the hero protector against those devilish demons that would harm another without any concern…
Like a super hero, I would defend the innocent,
The ones who struggle to defend themselves (like me).

Life is glorious, precious beyond imagination, no time to waste with meanness, abuse or selfish plans.

How DARE you???!!!

The part of me that's frozen seems to feel SO unsafe that I pause,
Stop - to protect the part of me that LONGS to soar so that I can stay ALIVE though
Frozen long enough to see if I can be true to my heart and LIVE – safe!

Sadly, I have come to a place where it seems I must be willing to do WHATEVER'S necessary to protect myself.

It's as if that's the price I hav'ta pay for freedom.

Hopefully, I can move on to a place where it doesn't feel like it has to be "them or me"
Cause it WILL be me!

I only wanted to find my voice,
Express my heart,
Explore me.

What gave you the idea that you could judge me, put your stuff on me, put me down, dismiss me, make light of me?!
Harm ME?

I only wanted to soar!

The infinite skies are big enough for everyone.

Demons: Everyone?

Super Hero: Yes! Every <u>single</u> one.

So! DON'T get in my way!

The Meaning of Jazz

My people are badass!
We create
Rap
Spin rhymes out of thing air
Smash & dunk spheres
Create melodies never repeating the same thing twice
Multiply the heartbeat exponentially with our drums
And tell stories of passion on the shins
of the animals we ate for dinner.
My people are bad ass
We create
Continuously unfolding life songs like magic pulsating
through our souls.

Who is this one?

Who is this one that when murdered, rises again
abused, beaten, destroyed
erupts as greatness
bringing its gifts to the world.
Stamped on, trampled into the dust, this one,
grows birds of paradise.

Who is this one
disparaged, denied, marginalized and ignored
that builds a matrix to climb upwards?

Who is this one – hated (envied really) and denigrated yet emotes LOVE.

This one, stolen from the depths of Africa…
Hmm…It must be the personification of God!

Toni Hamilton is driven by her love of creativity. A vocalist, first and foremost, Toni was hooked by the masters she grew up listening to – Ella, Sarah, Etta, Shirley, Johnny Hartman, Nat King Cole, Smokey, Cutis Mayfield, James Brown, Bill Withers, Donny Hathaway and Al Jarreau to name a few. A jazz singer first, she has performed as guest vocalist at Trumpets, the Lenox Lounge, Showman's, on jazz cruises and many other venues.

Deeply committed to spiritual practices, Toni sings and speaks at Centers for Spiritual Living and Unity churches in the North East.

Although she began writing poetry at an early age, she has recently reignited her quest to express her spirit using the depth and breadth of "words".

Toni caught the acting bug early on but it remained secondary to music. Her last role was in a production of the Vagina Monologues.

Toni has studied voice with Lewis McCollough, Danny Madden and Claude Stein. She studied acting with Brian MCEleny.

Most recently, Toni has been blessed with the ability to draw and paint. She is also working on a book to fill a void she dares not ignore.

K`larity K Johnson

ABOUT TIME...

Its hard to see clear through the rain
Its hard to smile pretty through the pain
Its hard to let go of loss & focus on the gain
Its hard to press on and do it again
Its hard to figure out where to begin
but Then...
Each movement shifts a bit more
Each moment has gifts in store
Each improvement holds tests to endure
Each empowerment reveals what it's all for
Each enjoyment reminisces on the before
but Then...
Your rain begins to slow
Your pain ceases to grow
Your gain increases from what you sow
Your again leads to another tomorrow
You're beginning to look beyond the sorrow
And Then...
HE lifts your head, reminds you what HE shed
Recalls what HE said
Seek the Kingdom & Speak with Wisdom
Understand HIS purpose in mind,
Because HIS Process is About Time

MIDNIGHT_WHISPERS

Silent screams of LOUD whispers
Neglected Emotions of untold lies
Disappearing with the sound, re-appearing in the peace
The stillness in the Appearance, displays in the lack of coherence
Being blinded, naive & clever, no longer bonded, un-tied together
Surpassing ALL understanding
Lost, deserted wanderer, Gazing at green grass over yonder
Taking in the ray's warm, swimming in the rain's storm
Sailing upstream, drifting on a dream, one of you & me – that can no longer be
Relentless & uptight, sleepless battles I fight (night after night)
Because your presence is STILL there
(I Swear) most times I still wish you were here
But then again, it doesn't really matter if you are far or near
Because when midnight whispers, I'll always shed a tear...
Maybe I'll cry one for every memory, each year, every promise, each kiss that lingers there
Or maybe I'll smile, sit awhile & remember the good times
The ones we shared building life, beats, & rhymes
Or maybe I'll dance and sing a song, laugh & pretend nothing is wrong
Hide my soul behind a mask of disillusion, Attempt to sort out this mass of confusion
Cause I aint got a clue, but I can't talk to you
(so now what am I suppose do?)
Well I can pick up & move on with my issues why
Or release them free, under a Moonlit sky

SOUL SEARCHING

Trying to fit your picture of Reality,
I lost my view and sense of Clarity
Feeling empty afterwards, going nowhere but backwards
I sat back and let time rewind, slowly playing itself out across my mind
I begin to recall when it all happened
The moment my life drifted and started collapsing
Searching for a place to belong
Searching in spaces that were all wrong
Searching for a place to be, but going nowhere
Searching for a space in me that was always hidden there
No longer lost & hateful inside, 'cause now I'm just grateful & filled with pride
To HIM I will always be thankful and try my hardest to remain true & faithful
I'm no longer in chains
I'm no longer ashamed
I'm no longer restrained
I'm no longer in pain
I'm no longer oppressed or contained
I'm now released to be ME; I'm now released to be FREE

In This Skin (BEAUTY)

Her name is Beauty but nobody knows/ It's hidden beneath and rarely shows
Sits under a dim light that barely glows / The thickness of her lips & the width of her nose
Wanting hair that flows, turns & sways / Ev'ry which way – when the wind blows
But tall & curvy, full & curly is the way it grows
Flaunted & displeased, taunted & teased –
that's the way it goes
So… again Her name is Beauty, but she still doesn't know
A strong image once deceived to be weak / A strong image once denied to speak
So she splits her verbs when she spits her words
Often taught she had no choice / Often thought she had no voice
Just image & sexuality, when in actuality / there was power in her mentality to birth Life into her reality
She didn't need false idols & role models / Her truth didn't exist on a box or inside a bottle
No, she was without borders & beyond waters / She refused to be used, as one of society's abandoned daughters
Spawning from disappointed mothers and distorted lovers who themselves were exploited by so many others
She refused to feel foreign in the land of her origin / Republican or Dem, before all of them
Were they, was She still an American, A Woman, too bold & too feminine
Right wing or left, Pro-life or Death
Liberal or Conservatism, Ownership or Plagiarism
This land is your land, In GOD we trust / But does His plan still have faith in us?
(in this atmosphere we've created so unfair & unjust)
Trading promises for ignorance / intelligence for intolerance
Mixed interpretations for fixed impersonations / intimidation exchanges with limitations
False campaigns & misused slogans / Pawns for friends & misused tokens

Beauty been sold & Beauty been sown – Beauty been given & Beauty been grown
YES, Beauty is twisted & often slurred / Beauty gets clouded & often blurred
Beauty gets turned & often tossed / Beauty gets burned & often gets lost
Beauty gets permed and often pressed / Beauty gets cut & often faded / Beauty gets diluted & often degraded
But when Beauty became natural & real / Beauty opened her heart & began to feel
She stared at her reflection, a thorough inspection / Seeing both the joy & the rejection
Seeing both the norm & the exception
Realizing that the truth had been a misconception / Translated from someone else's perception
Balancing her toughness with a need for protection / Masking her roughness with the need for correction
Her past foretells of days to come, she now walks to the beat of a different drum
Beauty stands & Beauty bends / Beauty expands & Beauty extends
Beauty wanted to be bold & free / Not what someone else told her to be
Beauty wanted to reflect passion & liberty / Not what someone else told her to see
She was independent & defiant / Confidant & reliant
Beauty became determined & focused / Beauty became determined to notice
All the facts mixed with the lies / All the acts fixed with compromise
All the answers with the questions why / Beauty started to explore & soar the skies
She didn't cross every 'T' or dot every 'I' / She didn't draw neat patterns or stay within the lines
She began to rethink & change her mind / Beauty in fact was often ahead of the time
Beauty paralleled between the revolution & the evolution
Beauty is a face that speaks from the grave / With eyes so strong & a spirit so brave
A force inside no course could contain

Shades of makeup, afraid to wake up / Cover girl or Maybeline, Harlot or Queen
For years Beauty's truth has gone un-seen
Ms. Elle, Mademoiselle or condemned Jezebel
Her ebony essence unveils a sweet honey layered presence
Beauty is now Upscale with her own enterprise / to her amazement but no surprise
From the crown of her cuticles / She was always soft & beautiful
Beauty is dark & lovely with only GOD above thee
A shining light that evolves continuously / A guiding light that revolves endlessly
Beauty has a name that's loud & proud / Beauty went against the grain & outside the crowd
She saw so much from the outside in / She saw so much hurt from where it begins
She saw so much pain trapped within – but then
She saw so much freedom, just consciously being, in her GOD given skin.

Evolutionary Soldier

I spit for the un-sung warrior, the over-looked & ignored soldier
The ones with ALL guts -but no glory, the strong voices of an untold story
The trailblazers of the beaten path, the hell-raisers left in the aftermath
The one + ONE = 3 to none, The undefined- "classified", without an Add
(a history erased & all they had)
So I emerged from the ash, with the Panther & The Lash
It's evolutionary, so I redefined the dictionary
I proceed, spring forth from the seed -- of a Revolutionary
Cause essentially, they want us all gone eventually
"if I ruled the world" & reigned from the throne
I raise my fist for solidarity to exist...take back & reclaim my Own (people)
Who've been denied, wept & died, deceived & connived---by evil
YES! I am she, descended from he, an external extension & connection of "we"
The few & the many, the chosen & unsure...the remnant of plenty, the stolen souls washed a 'shore
The starved & the hungry, the tired & the thirsty--those whose name lay claim to un-worthy
The head-less horsemen, midnight watchmen- that move in the night, by the light provided
Go-get'rs & Flow spitters, Verbal Assassins & un-veiled Black masked men
Plots & Schemes, this "American" dream is more to endure than what it seems
So I fight til it changes & I write to re-arrange it
Lyrically & Mentally cause Spiritually it was written & therefore meant to be
I AM daily HIStory, not one month & lunar days a calendar year that sooner fades
I speak with the heart of those who dared & cared to be brave
Stood their ground, Stood tall & Stood proud
and refused to be silent when the violent were loud

I talk up for them who couldn't talk back, I walk for them who were often sent back
To the end of the line---
so I'll keep speaking for 'em & writing the rhyme-
Elevating souls & liberating minds until the end of Time.

The Queen

Where can you find the Queen?
Well, the Queen can be seen in the beauty of nature.
The Queen can be heard when the wind blows.
The Queen can be felt when love touches your heart.
The Queen can be observed performing the "gift of life"
The Queen can be mighty among few
or stand out among the crowds.
The Queen can be down
or simply down the block, around-the-way.
The Queen moves swiftly yet with careful steps, while changing her environment.
The Queen reigns within the community while campaigning our causes around the world – for it is her empire.
The Queen nurtures the mind of her King & cultivates the soil of her young.
Made of the ashes and dusts of the earth,
yet more valuable than worth.
She's a hard rock, strong stone, can't be broken because she holds her own!
Like rubies & diamonds the Queen is a jewel, though many seek to refine her, others try to define her,
still our society denies her!
Instead, we settle for a cheap imitation , man-made lab creation of a gem, when all the while she's been dwelling among them!
The Queen is not boastful but she's proud,
She's proud of her legacy that tells of her greatness.
Descended from the heavens, manifested from the womb, knows all because she's been here before
Yet with each journey she leaves behind something new ... something wonderful.

So while the world slept she made some thousands upon thousands of warriors that will continue on her name
It's an uneven number, so it's odd to say that from one , many remain.
But when you question her existence,
rest assured that she is real,
For the Queen was just with you, but if you blink too fast, you just missed her.

MS- Fortune

They have 'subtracted' HER to balance the equation
SHEs reduced from the 'whole' number, like a mere fraction
Applications of algebraic rules, Tests & Theories conducted with barbaric tools
Replaced numbers for 'X's , Abbreviated like "txts", Tallying the marks to HER exit
Constructing stories from the Nurturing-Nature of a Nursery; Esteem built from Legos
Jagged placement like a puzzle piece create a pictured punctured like deflated egos
Never taught to fully adorn HER halo', Forced to reform friends from Barbies to G.I. Joes
Overzealous dreamer, in search of a believer, but instead they Demean HER!
Their demeanor is to lean HER into placing "high goals" to aim for what's ---beneath HER!
Sight set on the pearl-Moon between her thighs, because society's Solar Eclipse has blocked the eye to HER pain, HER screams, HER cries.
HER voice echoes under chalk lines, tilting the greater scale to less than equal signs
SHE is the shifted focus of reality that exists
within HER mind,
It is there that SHE can find --- the square root, the Influence of HER existence is divided into
multiple places of truth.
Daring to search for the common denominator, SHE has

become the chosen numerator, future liberator – of the past.
While HER future is presently visible,
in every factor SHE is indivisible.
Solid statue and hard to replace HER, so they try to Trace
HER – with impure intent to de-face HER
Missing the details, so it indeed fails to completely erase HER
– with impure intent to utterly disgrace HER.
HER words have been imitated, Vision falsely duplicated,
making HER mission all the more complicated.
Seeing he that have an ear, turn deaf from fear, so SHE's
overcome from so far that SHE's still strong & still here!
Smooth swerve when SHE steer 'cause SHE got lots in HER
trunk bringing up the rear
Equipped with shield, sword, & spear, HER vehicle
totes sharecropped fields, musical soul, whips & chains,
outhoused-stained anguish & pain, auction blocks of
empires brought to shame, Sea-sickness, mental depression,
hollow drums & dances of rain, Cotton Gins & sunflower
seeds, doubledutch ropes & colorful hair beads, homeland
Liberation, homegoing celebration, home of yesterday future
generation –
Yes, SHE smooth with the swerve when it's HER turn to
steer, carrying junk in the trunk and dropping it Here!
Defamed HER character with black-face contortionist, the
twisted view of an contaminated cartoonist; Painted in Green
and bedazzled with Bling placing "Polly" before crackers to
get HER to sing, but when the cage was bent open SHE took
flight to spread HER wings.
So SHE is Not sorry, SHE does Not apologize, SHE will Not
conform to the Norm' as a disguise!
SHE will Not be quiet, SHE will Not sit down or cross HER
palms neatly!
SHE will Not walk softly, SHE will Not step aside, SHE will
not turn down & "act" more sweetly!
She will Not give you a pass or let your *ish slide, SHE will
Not run away, cower or hide!
She can Not dumb it down or speed it up, SHE will No
Longer accept it – SHE's had enough!

She will Not stop talking fast (because they listen to slow), SHE will NOT shift the Light to deflect HER glow, SHE will not divulge the secrets of all SHE's knows!
She will NOT stop using "ethnic" names, nor refer to her children as such – and wishes you do the same!
She will NOT "blend in", cover up, or change...
SHE will NOT forget HERstory nor the reason why it must remain.

Ms. Mo Klarity hails from New York City. She attended Norfolk State University, in Norfolk Virginia. Klarity has been writing and sharing poetry since the age of thirteen. Her works have been featured in several online and print publications, as well as a poetic anthology.

LaTasha Boyd Jones

RUTH:
Partly Equitable with a Chance of Reciprocity

She awakened
Blooming
Stretching her petals
    Far & wide—
Transfigured.

There is a Woman
Birthing Messiah,
Naming her King,
Yet waiting—
Waiting for a man to tell her when time comes.

There is a Woman
Singing hymns—
Touching hems,
And yet,
Waiting for him to heal her.

There is a Woman
Packing five loaves & two fish,
Weaving weight's wealth outta cents,
Still,
Waiting for a man to feed them.

There is a Woman
Conjuring Peace,
Anointing feet,
Lacking *no*thing,
Shalom—
Yet, She waits to take up her bed & walk.

There is a Woman
spillin' laafta,
remindin' sista— "Weeping may endure the night,"
But joy comesaftamournin'.
comes afta mournin'
afta mournin'
mornin' —*selah*.

There is a Woman
Dwelling in the Depths—Her
Womb whispering,
Sheltering Secrets,
Mobilizing Missions,
Preserving Promises,
Breathing Life,
Treading Water,
Balancing Worlds,
Between her thighs —
holdingtheson
who never asked permission.

There is a Woman

She,
Her.

Ruth Rising
by name,
book,
An assignment

Ashes in the Sky.

Lines Un/Broken:
Pyramids. *Plantations.*
<u>Projects</u>. ~~Penitentiaries~~.

Who knows better than WE, America?
We went from Pyramids to Plantations,
to Projects to Penitentiaries, and
 you think America changed for me?

Pyramids.

We rose as whispers shaped in stone,
Through every grain, our spirits shone.

Etched by the Nile, kissed by the flame.
Eternity crowned us by our name.

The sun draped us in golden threads,
From deserts vast where Kings have led.

Our shadows stretched to speak with the stars.
We built the heavens, listening to the gods.

Obelisks, unbroken and unbowed,
Standing firm when darkness shrouds.

Our tips ignite the endless skies.
Our light burns: it never dies.

We were snatched from pyramids,
dragged to plantations in chains,
stripped of our names, our tongues restrained.
We went from Pyramids to Plantations,
to Projects to Penitentiaries and
you think America's changed?

Plantations.

The Earth drank tears from stolen dreams,
a crimson tide beneath the plow.
Our cries became morning streams,
yet hope still blossomed on each bough.

They cast our bodies into chains;
these roots run deep beneath their feet.
The hymns of sorrow moaned with pain;
we turned despair to fields of wheat.

Stolen gold stained with sweat and sin,
Still, we sang beneath the moon.
Each note defied the lash's grin;
our hearts beat loud, a sacred tune.

**We went from
Pyramids to
Plantations, to
Projects to
Penitentiaries.**

Projects.

The white coats came with needles sharp,
and played their scalpel like a harp.

Their needles wove scars in flesh and bone;
Black bodies still hold tales of stolen thrones.

They called us vessels, machines built for pain;
with royal blood running through our veins.

Dreams dissected for power's thrill;
scars studied with ink and quills.

A legacy sacred, a sacrifice penned on scrolls,
escape the cage unbound our souls,

warning etched for future eyes;
our essence soaring past their lies.

**We went from
Pyramids to
Plantations, to
Projects, to
Penitentiaries.
America tested our tenacity and
poisoned our plight, but God's Promises
always blaze bright.**

~~Penitentiaries.~~

The fields of green became gray walls,
where shadows whispered of despair.
Yet freedom danced through prison halls,
Her voice, Harriett, alights the morning air.

The bars they forged could not confine
a beacon guiding the spirit born of royal fire.
Through cracks in stone, our dreams align,
ascending high, a boundless choir.

Though numbered suits adorned our frame,
our names carved stars across the night.
From every cell, we stoked the flame;
resistance burned with endless light.

From Pyramids to Plantations, to Projects to Penitentiaries—we are covered by God's panoply.

From stone to chains, from steel to song,
We learned the language and remixed our song.
Its heart, its rhythm, its endless ties,
The spiral turns, but—we always rise.
Our scars fill crowns; our pain refines gold,
Through every era, valued, strong, and bold.
We've claimed the future, spanned the years,
With fabric stitched from toil and tears.
The eternal flame defies the tide; with ancestors, we rise.
Carving our likeness in treasures beyond the skies.
We are the pulse of nations, the Earth's refrain.
Unbroken and Unbowed: Royal, we remain.

Tasha Jones is a celebrated poet, writer, educator, and cultural advocate known for infusing everyday life experiences with scripture and poignant storytelling. Described as having "the soul of Nikki Giovanni draped in the haute couture fashions of a runway model," her poetry explores themes of love, loss, resilience, and empowerment, resonating deeply with audiences worldwide.

She hosts *In the Beginning: The Spoken Word Podcast*, the #1 podcast in its genre, and serves as the editor of *Poems & Parables*, a literary journal amplifying Black voices. Tasha's writing includes the highly anticipated *Pyramids. Plantations. Projects. Penitentiaries*, a profound exploration of identity, history, and the transformative power of language, with a foreword by the late Dan Wakefield.

A TEDx Fellow and Reginald L. Jones Fellow at the *Indianapolis Recorder*, Tasha is also the author of *Hello Beautiful*, which inspired the "Hello Beautiful Movement," empowering youth through the power of words. Her work has been featured in *The Nation* and *Essence*, and she is a sought-after speaker, performer, strategist, curriculum writer, thinker, and educator.

Tasha lives in Indianapolis with her children, Shalom and Messiah. Connect with her on social media @iamtashajones.

Pharoah Davis - P.O.D.

Summary of Montgomery

Just a brief summary of what went down in Montgomery
On the 5th day of Black August...when we all saw this
Act of Black unity in defense against White insanity
Exhibiting deficiencies in humanity
So we being hospitable... made it possible
For them to be transported to the precinct or hospital
Which-ever entity could remedy their sickness...
We bear witness to the fact that Woke Blackness has each-others back
Black August... when we remember Black resistance
Freedom fighters, activist, and political prisoners
So on this 5th day, a 19th century style riverboat...
Named the Harriot carried some free minded folk...
Who came to free a Black man from the bandage of White rage
White rage is was set the stage for the Black signal to go off
And so like the Bat signal... the Black hat was tossed
Cause when the peaceful Pickett wasn't met with peace
Levels of racial tension began to increase
Black feet... all up in white asses... caught on video & viewed by the masses
A Freestyle beat down on the dock...
in honor of 50 years of hip hop
Sometimes picket signs and protest lines
are the means of change
But on this day the only Picket
was brother Dame's last name
That's Damion Pickett, assumed to be a security guard
But the Harriot's Co-captain is his title and job
So in this summary of Montgomery
Let's briefly breakdown the history
In my research I've found, that everything went down
Right there at 'Montgomery's Court square'
One of the main Slave trading post
On the whole east coast... of this nation
For generations... many of us came from

Right off the ship into that 'Montgomery Warehouse'
Where they would inspect us...
and prep us before bringing us out & marching us down
Commerce street...
Where We... were the commerce
We the goods & services bought and sold
as the traders converse
And bid... there at the auction Block
From the Boat to the Dock...There at *Court square*
So Montgomery Blacks were always clear
And never disillusioned about our exclusion
from America's idea of first class citizens
This is how it's been... even considering
The strides that've been made
The foundations laid
Like the acts of Black pride... in 1955
When the civil rights movement came alive
With Rosa and the buses they didn't ride
Together for 380 days... thru the efforts of the M.I.A...
.Montgomery Improvement Association...
Inspired by Marcus Garvey's organization... U.N.I.A.
They improved their situation
From December 5 to August 5... with 68 years in between
When Woke folk are poked the ancestors are invoked... or so it seems
Whether 380 days of a boycott
Or 380 seconds of a white ass whipping at the dock
Montgomery has some history of being Woke
From the ships... to the Bus... to the boat
From the Auction block... to the Bus Boycott... to the Harriot's Dock
In summary, it seems Willie never made it to Montgomery
Willie must've missed the boat and Buses weren't running
He was never able to come and further divide
the black mentality and cultural pride
of the African Alabamians
The Montgomery, Masai, Niabengi, Nubians
From the ship... to the dock they never stopped
holding on to our integrity...Down there Montgomery.
This is just my summary

The Water Broke

The water broke and the birthing
of the African American began
Starting from an encounter between two...
Africa and Europe
The nurturer and the deceiver
The foreigner who seems to come in peace
only comes to steal, kill, and colonize right before our eyes
This diseased deceiver showed up on the shores of our home
with a bag of lies, as soulless eyes tell stories
 of a god that dies on a cross and of course we are captivated
and then held captive
And this captivity led to the Raping of our purity
Raped and impregnated by the white Seamen who traveled
far and long to reach the egg, the nest
The fertile lands of Africa, the cradle of the world
And the Semen fermented itself
in the nest of our mother- land
in the womb of the world.
And we were conceived...
carried in the belly of the Bautista
The belly of the good ship Jesus, belly of the Clotilda
For months, in the waters of mother- earth
And the water broke when we arrived as new beings
Born through the pains of labor,
free labor pains of countless hours,
Upon days, upon decades, upon centuries
We were delivered onto a soil of unfamiliar ground
Given a new name,
new language, and a new god.
With a new father, a pirate father who rapes us again
Even after we've been here
Created into this new people
Only to be misused and abused
The Water broke
The Water broke birthing us into Hell
and yet we still survive the scorching torture of Hell's fire
The water broke as we sing 'wade in the water' in the day
But we wade in the waters at night

so the dogs can't follow the scent
The water broke when our Moses named Harriet
parted the swamps and the creeks to free our people
The Water broke
when the Jim crow water hoses broke loose on us
while we peacefully pray and protest against the injustices
against us
The water broke when the levy's broke
When the levy's were blown up and broken on purpose
to overflow in our hood and not theirs
The water broke in Flint's filtration system
As our families are poisoned by toxins

The Water broke in 2019...
As the 400th anniversary
of our birth as enslaved African Americans...
The unwanted guest, as opposed to welcomed citizens
who happen to have built these cities, roads and
bridges over the troubled waters.
The Water Broke
The water is our means of survival
Without it there is no life
There is no oxygen, there is no us
We must fix the water so that no one else can break it
As we are the water of life
We are the water of this world
And we quench the thirst of all who drink from our creations,
our existence
The brilliance of us can create a new birth of beauty and well
being
Once we collect, filtrate and distribute our own water of life
Then and only then will the Water be Fixed.

Creatively Black

Black is the foundation from which all is birthed. From the Black universe... to the rich Black dirt... the soil of the earth. Black people born and birthed, nurtured and nursed...in the land of their Mother... Africa, then migrated to other parts of the Earth. We...the first ones on the scene. But what does it all mean?   And how is this information essential?

   Well, for one... it lets us know our true potential. If our ancestors were masters of the land... then there is nothing we can't over-stand. We are the original people, coming from the original clan.   If our ancestors made substantial contributions to history... then it's only natural to know that, so can we.

If no one told you that you could fly... then you would spend your life on the ground looking at the sky...with desires to soar and explore the clouds but not knowing why.But a creative mind aligned with the Spirit is a mind that is free... And it seems to be the time to remind us of who we used to be. So let us spread our wings and take flight. Soar across the Atlantic retracing the route of the middle passage. Soar across the Nile valley into the heart of Cairo... Then fly to the top of Mount Kilimanjaro.
And rest upon that rock atop of the tallest peak in Africa... While looking across at the face of the Sphinx made in the likeness of King Khafre.
Let us stand tall and strong upon that stone, that foundation... of ages... written in the pages of every scripture ever compiled... Our story, evolved from the Nile, with a culture that paved ways for our ancestors to pave way for us.
We, the ones kissed by the sun... with an abundance of melanin, have always been Creative... That's not something we do, that's how we live. We, who live creatively... are the epitome of creativity. We, the creators of civilization... We created the blueprint on how to create a Nation. We, are the soil of the earth. And just like the black dirt, from which a plethora of colors are birthed. From green grass... To orange weeds. Purple flowers under brown trees... with red apples

and auburn leaves. And all of the colorful vegetables...
Orange yams to yellow squash.... As we even knew how to
use the dirt to wash, the gold, silver, diamonds and rubys
which create the aesthetic of glittering Black dirt... Just like
the stars up against the Black Universe. Yes, all colors come
from Black... The Brown, Red, Yellow, Baige, and White, in
fact... Every color of man on earth... Thru the Black of Africa,
he was birthed. So,We know the power of Black that lives
within... the universe, the earth, and our own skin. This is
where all life begins.
Life is what we love to give. So ...Creative...That's not what
we do, that's how we live.   And as a matter of fact... We are
Black Creations...
That's **Creatively Black.**

Another Brown

Another Brown...
Down
Another Brown man
Gunned down by the Boys in blue
Not the crips... This blue is darker
Harder to detect... They're suppose to serve and protect.
But some of their members

have their own agendas.

And now another Brown is down...

Another Black shot in the back

by this blue blooded pack of beast...

Leaving black and brown bodies dead in the streets...

Giving Black men a bitter dose of defeat

until we rise to our feet and stand up to this beast

Universal law says you have the human right

to protect your life and life of loved ones

by any means necessary, said Brother Malcolm

It is necessary to defend, regardless the outcome.
Warriors must remember their mission
Ancestors are screaming if we listen
we can hear their command and instruction
We must anticpate the fate of Destruction
for this empire.
For there is another that awaits...
But it can not be Erected
until our mission is directed,
our family protected,
Our people respected... by us...first
Then the curse will be lifted
As the enemy's foot lifted
from off our necks by our hands...
as every Black Man, woman and child will stand
and participate in the solution...
It is our Fate...the time is NOW for REVOLUTION
Those who know their destiny, have little fear.
We are at war... is this not clear?
Death to any Demon that seemingly
threatens the life of this special breed.
We the example for the world to feed... from.
We the people of the SUN...
As our skin absorbs it,
our hair grows towards it.
And those that envy, trick us
into thinking they ignore it.
But no, it's too late
We now understand the hate.
It's been obvious from the beginning up to date
From the Dreams of Martin...

King and Trayvon
To the Screams of Brown...
James and Michael
whether singing or dying we can feel that pain
of ancient souls crying through
We know what we must do
We can no longer play around
We will no longer tolerate another Brown to go down.
Not another Black on his back...
by this blue blooded pack of beast.
We must organize at least
retaliate at best
while the beast rest
in his safe little home
We strategize through revolutionary poems
Whether the Fruit of Islam, The Drop squad,
or New Deacons of Defense...
The New Black Panthers, A Balck miltia
or a group of brothers with common sense.
We pledge if there is a neighborhood watchmen
or a racist rogue cop
that unjustly takes a life
then their heartbeat must stop.
Today we stand and claim our ground
No more will we tolerate ANOTHER BROWN... DOWN

Poet Please

Let's pour out a libation
for the Creations of the poet
With their rhythms & sounds... in leaps & bounds
Personal notes & endless quotes
The flow of poetry brings sounds of serenity to my soul
I hear music in the words spoken
Heard with my 3rd ear open,
sounding as clear as my own voice
Talking sense back into my mind when it seems I've lost it
At times I find clarity as the words move melodically
Thru my ear-drumming in my mind...Tapping into my soul
And I am moved by the grammatical groove
creating a melodic mood
The words are music... and like soul food I use it to feed on
Getting my groove on...
But We... who dance are often called crazy
by those who cannot hear the music
So Po it please! Po the wine. Pour the libation
For those who laid the foundation before
Let us pour it please. Pour some for the Poet Tree
That tree which provides shelter and shade
And fruit from its branches... feeding us with answers
The poet tree. Let us pour it please.
As the words are water... we pour onto the tree to sustain it
As it sustains us
And the poet tree is for the poor who need more
than just dictation of what and what not to do
thru fallible stories... We need parables of glory to make us
think for ourselves
Those words nurture our mental health
and inspire spiritual wealth
And ignite our imagination...Let us pour a libation for the
poet with words of brilliance from yesterday, tomorrow and
this very hour. Words are power
So let us Po it Please
Pour out a little Rum...
for those who used the pen as their drum
 From Paul Laurence to Langston...

from Audre Lorde to Gwendolyn,
Po it please!!! For Phyliss Wheatly & Lucy Terry.
For Maya, Margaret, & Mari Evans.
For Amiri and Gil still spitting gems from heaven
Po it please!... Even for those who are still on the grind
Like Sonia, Nikki & The Last Poets of our time
And we find this masterful art
to be an integral part of humanity
Like the roots of a poet tree connecting we the people
Poetry has touched and inspired me...
Poetry has taken me higher
So I can see things from a different view
When the word hits, my soul sits...
right there in that pew digesting the sermon
Constantly learning and yearning to be enlightened once again
When I listen to Wordsmiths with the gift of the pen
Or even spoken off the top with metaphors dropped in the
verse with no need to curse
Cause the vocabulary is extensive like Rakim
One of them poetic rappers who perfected the blend.
Blending of rap & poetry
which has a history of flowing naturally
as the relation has always been.
The Art transcends the titles given
From Rapper to Rhymer to Lyricist...
to Cultural journalist or Wordsmith
From Griot to Muse to Ghetto stenographer...
 Preacher or Prophet or Lyrical videographer
The poet is everything from Soothsayer
to the Slick word player
And even the love songwriters who set it up
for the baby way makers
However we choose to define the poet... just know it...
is a craft mastered
From watching & listening and sometimes questioning
The actions of birds & bees, humans and trees
Or the fall of rain or a warm summer breeze
 So let every living thing that has breath give praise to...
The Poet Please!!!

Pharoah Davis - P.O.D.

Born 1968 and raised in Queens, N.Y. Pharoah is a poet, songwriter, playwright, screenwriter, author, historian and teacher. As the product of two parents who are educators, Pharoah has an appreciation for education as a student and educator. Listening to stories and firsthand accounts of the segregated, *Jim Crow,* south told to him by his grandparents, gave him a deeper understanding and appreciation for Black life in America. He is the son of one of an acclaimed poet (Abiodun Oyewole of 'The Last Poets') Pharoah attended (*HBCU*) Benedict College in Columbia, South Carolina. He did his last years of college at City College of New York where he received his B.A. degree in African American studies. Pharoah started a four man singing group named *Asante.* The group was signed to Columbia records in the mid 1990's. He is a proud dad of 6 and resides in Fort worth, Texas.
Pharoah Oyewole Davis

Pharoahsarmy2@gmail.com
682 313 1277 cell

The Pledge

I want to be what I can be
To be proud, healthy and FREE
I want to say what I know
To help my brothers and sisters GROW
I want to feel good about me
And blame no one for my MISERY
I'll be strong, turn it around
I want to go up, I'm not going DOWN
I want to do what I can do
To make all my dreams come TRUE
Remember my past, the good and bad
How I make art, even when it was SAD
I want to share whatever my gift
And when you're feeling low I'll give you A LIFT
I want to live without FEAR
And know that I'm blessed for being HERE
And know that you're blessed for being HERE
And know that we're blessed for being HERE
And know that we are BLESSED

Abiodun Oyewole

www.ingramcontent.com/pod-product-compliance
Lightning Source LLC
Chambersburg PA
CBHW071203160426
43196CB00011B/2178